Embracing the Journey

Between Edenville and Eternity

KARMEN ASCH

authorHOUSE®

AuthorHouse™
1663 Liberty Drive
Bloomington, IN 47403
www.authorhouse.com
Phone: 1-800-839-8640

First published by AuthorHouse 9/1/2010

ISBN: 978-1-4490-1124-6 (sc)
ISBN: 978-1-4490-1125-3 (e)

Printed in the United States of America

This book is printed on acid-free paper.

Dedicated to my mentor and friend,
Pastor Larry Starke.
Thank you for teaching me almost everything
I know ~ especially for showing me the
most important truth: how to develop a
relationship with my Heavenly Father.
I am forever grateful!

To borrow the title of a song:
**"The Road Goes on Forever
and the Party Never Ends"**
~ when you're a child of God!

Book Contents/Article Titles

Chapter Three – HOPE

Chapter Four – PEACE

Chapter Five – WORSHIP

Chapter Six – PRAYER

Acknowledgments

I have so many people to thank for helping me write the articles in this book, I cannot possibly name them all. To my friends, family and co-workers: you have no idea how significant your influence has been on my life over the years! You have blessed my life more than you will ever know - thank you!

Here is a list of a few that have greatly affected me: Special thanks to Karen Zeitz (AKA "Mom") for proofreading my final draft! From early on, my mom trained me in the use of grammar, challenging me to always increase my vocabulary and pushing me to write letters to grandparents, aunts and uncles when I was very young. I believe this helped me express myself and develop creative ways to entertain others with my writing. I grew up attending Hillside Elementary and my 4th grade teacher, "Mrs. Kelly", had us keep journals. She was the first to tell me, "Someday you're going to write a book!" Thank you, Nancy, for that inspiration - I never forgot it. Later, my hilarious 5th grade teacher, Mrs. Porter, allowed me and another student to write poetry for our class and post it in the hallway, increasing my love for "creative writing".

I am generally a quiet person and as a young adult I needed encouragement not only in expressing myself, but in gaining self-confidence. The following people helped me develop the self-esteem I needed to begin making quality decisions: I met Pastor Larry Starke when I was 15 years old – and I've dedicated this book to him for his powerful influence in my life. He was one of the first people who took the time to let me talk to him about things that concerned me. He listened to me like he really cared about me and set an excellent example for me, showing me how to talk to God as my Heavenly Father – and also explained how to hear God speak to my heart. This was the most beneficial lesson I learned. It has carried me through the tough times growing up and helped me determine who I wanted to be when I grew up! By learning to pray, I saw His hand at work in my life and experienced His great love, grace and mercy – and realized there is a purpose for me.

Another person who helped motivate me to set higher goals is Mrs. McGinnis, my high school science teacher. She recommended me for a "Project SEED" job at Central Michigan University in the summer of 1988, before my senior year in high school. That job provided a wonderful opportunity for me to branch out socially when I was just 16 years old, and I really needed that! Dr. Mohanty, the professor I worked for at CMU, helped me tremendously as I worked under his direction in the Organic Chemistry lab. Graduate students, Peter Balanda and Atul Bhatnagar, were also very friendly, helpful and influential and actually caused me to reconsider my plans after high school, encouraging me to attend college. The summer that I worked in the science lab at CMU helped shape my future more than I realized at the time. It led to a part time co-op position at Dow Corning, and eventually a full time job. I'm grateful for the co-workers I've had the pleasure of working alongside: people of integrity that make work fun and have also become good friends – like a family. I also have enjoyed the international travel opportunities this job has provided.

In 2007, Ken Cline encouraged me to write more and gave me the vision to publish this book, containing my writings. He taught me that writing is a gift I will have to give an account for, and that we receive gifts from our Heavenly Father primarily to share with others.

Probably one of the biggest lessons in teaching me how to express myself came from my husband, Steve Asch. Through his encouragement and unconditional love for me, I learned how to share exactly what is on my mind - and after eight years of marriage, he says he has taught me too well!

Of course, my greatest appreciation is to my Heavenly Father, who designed me to love writing and blessed me over the years with a life filled with colorful experiences. I could write so many stories! He has given me the desires of my heart, before I even realized what those desires were! He has also weaved my life along a unique journey which led me to write this book, and perhaps more in the future.

I hope you enjoy this book. It is a compilation of "life lessons" that I have learned - either first-hand or from watching others experience "stuff". I realize I still have a lot to learn! I like to grow through the everyday experiences while here on earth. To quote Pastor Larry, "Life is a series of tests. If you pass the test, you won't have to take it again." I like to pass the more difficult tests the first time, so I'm learning to apply what I know and make the best decisions I can. If I fail, then I take the lesson that I've learned and apply it next time so I don't have to re-take the test.

Intro

I've often struggled on and off with how to balance my life having an serious dislike for the religious spirit – prideful, self-righteous people (like the Pharisees and Sadducees in the bible) who follow traditions but do not know how to love others unconditionally, and who are actually embarrassing to be associated with – and my unhindered love for God's grace and the truth He provides, as well as the wisdom and knowledge He offers to any who will continue to seek Him with all their ability.

This book offers some analogies in life that I hope point to the latter. I know how real God has been to me, but I also know many who struggle with seeing that in their own life – and I don't know why life seems so much easier for some than it is for others.

I think the principles taught to us in God's truth - His "love letter" to us, the bible - has a lot to do with finding contentment in a simple life of obedience to Him, while still having "freedom" to be all that we were created to. It's hard to explain, but it seems like it gets easier and easier to hear His voice and follow His direction as we continue our walk with Him.

So, I write to three groups of people: One is an audience of those who have not yet experienced the peace, joy and unbelievable love that He offers. I hope this book expresses that life in a way that draws you to seek Him for your benefit here on earth and for eternity.

Another group of people reading this book may know of God, but something is missing and you want to know Him more, to have that meaningful, personal and fulfilling relationship with Him.

For the third group of readers, I hope to encourage you to continue on – those of you who already know this great love, this exciting adventure with its fulfilling benefit package and abundant way of living. Keep moving forward!

Chapter One – GRACE

Be Real

But He said to me, "My grace is sufficient for you, for My power is made perfect in weakness." Therefore I will boast all the more gladly about my weaknesses, so that Christ's power may rest on me. That is why, for Christ's sake, I delight in weaknesses, in insults, in hardships, in persecutions, in difficulties. For when I am weak, then I am strong. (II Corinthians 12:9-10)

On my drive into work the other morning, I passed an interesting flock of turkeys in a field. The toms (males) had their tail feathers all fanned out to impress and attract the hens. Something peculiar caught my attention and out of curiosity, I looked again to fully capture the view in more detail. One of the toms had a significant chunk of his tail feathers missing, obviously from a near death experience. I imagined the scene as some predator walked away, disappointed with only a few feathers to snack on.

Still, this turkey proudly exposed his remaining tail feathers for the entire world to see. It was a humorous sight – and as I thought about it, a metaphor came to mind. How often do we try to "hide" our imperfections, hoping nobody will see we're not perfect? We like to share our strengths with others, but we dance around our weaknesses hoping nobody will notice we have any. I find it encouraging that God has told us that His strength is made perfect in our weaknesses – but I don't often apply that scripture to my own life and let myself be transparent to others. There is an inner pride that resists baring those things in our life that we wish didn't exist.

People can sense sincerity – there's no point trying to pretend we're perfect. We need to be real if we want to encourage others to experience the abundant life that Jesus offers. So, let's follow the example of that turkey and "boast in our weaknesses" so Jesus can be glorified!

Psalm 9:10 (AMP) – "And they who know Your name [who have experience and acquaintance with Your mercy] will lean on and confidently put their trust in You, for You, Lord, have not forsaken those who seek (inquire of and for) You [on the authority of God's Word and the right of their necessity]."

Spider Webs

"For since the creation of the world, God's invisible qualities - His eternal power and divine nature - have been clearly seen, being understood from what has been made, so that men are without excuse." (Romans 1:20)

One morning on my commute to work in the summer, I noticed something truly spectacular in the median along the expressway that I had never seen before. I was traveling east just as the sun lit up the morning sky. A morning mist had settled and heavy dew saturated everything – because of the sunrise and dew that morning, outlines of marvelous designs were magnificently highlighted. The awesome view captured my attention for nearly thirty miles as I couldn't stop gazing toward the weeds. Each one was decorated with a uniquely designed spider web!

Thousands, maybe millions, of spider's webs were exposed by the moisture and light that morning. It was like an invisible message had been made apparent and I could see the beautiful display that had been there all along.

Part of my amazement was the sheer beauty and number of webs; another source of my excitement was the thought "I've never seen this before. I never knew they existed!" For twenty years I've traveled along this way and I never knew I was passing by thousands of beautiful designs - and they're everywhere, not just along that highway! That's how it is with God's plan in our lives. On very rare occasions we capture a glimpse of the beauty He has designed in and around our life, but most of the time we are really unaware of what He is doing. Many times we wonder if He is doing anything at all - if He even knows we exist. But He is always at work behind the scenes.

I just finished reading "The Grand Weaver" by Ravi Zacharias, so this memory of the spider web scene resurfaced in my mind. It reminds of just how awesome God's plans are and of how closely He wants to work with us in our lives. He is interested in every detail of our life! He blesses us by using us as His vessels when we talk to Him, listen and obey Him. He gives us the opportunity to watch life unfold and see Him work His purposes.

"God denies a Christian nothing, but with a design to give him something better." (Richard Cecil)

Second Chances

"He who has an ear, let him hear what the Spirit says to the churches. To him who overcomes, I will give the right to eat from the tree of life, which is in the paradise of God." (Revelation 2:7)

Many of us have experienced – and naturally with much appreciation – a second chance. "Seabiscuit" and "Cinderella Man" are two movies, among many others, about society during the Great Depression. When given a second chance, something within us compels us to succeed, no matter what the cost - overwhelmingly grateful for the newfound opportunity. A familiar picture is clearly painted for us in each story.

Seabiscuit is a horse whose stature is too small and attitude too wild – and yet he is chosen by a trainer who sees beyond the apparent physical deficiencies. As a result of this second chance, Seabiscuit far exceeds everyone's expectations in winning races across the nation. In Cinderella Man, James Braddock is a boxer with a string of bad luck. His manager sees potential in him and goes out on a limb to support his training. In the end, going against all odds, Braddock wins the title. Because of the economic strain at the time, both characters become "heroes" to the viewing public who have an intense desire for their own second chance - and imagine their own success if given the opportunity. In each case, there is someone who sees the hidden potential and chooses to invest in them and another who trains them for excellence within their talent. One of the famous lines in Seabiscuit is "You don't throw away a whole life just 'cause its banged up a little." All of us have been "banged up a little" by life. But we also have One who knows our potential and invests in us. Our Heavenly Father has gifted each of us and given us His Holy Spirit who "trains" us in the way we need to go to fulfill our purpose here. Nothing is impossible as long as we are trusting in His strength. Psalm 28:7 says "The Lord is my strength and my shield; my hearts trusts in Him, and I am helped. Therefore my heart rejoices, and I praise Him with my song."

I often wonder what it is within a person that makes them continue on, and go above and beyond mediocrity to achieve greater things in life. Especially when I am feeling exhausted with life and my mind tends to focus on lack and hopelessness. I am grateful because I know I have been given a second chance. I know I can trust my Heavenly Father because I can look back at all He has done for me in the past - I have always been able to trust Him, even when I didn't know it until I was past the difficulty - He was there all along, making impossible situations work out in my favor. In times of transition and shifting, I find peace knowing that God never changes - He is the same yesterday, today and forever. There is comfort in realizing that every good and perfect gift comes from my Heavenly Father who provides me with everything I need. He knows what I need better than I do, and His supplies will never run out. The way He chooses to meet my needs may change, but His character remains the same. I know I have lots more to learn about His character, but I know that I can always trust Him in all things. I just need to remember to keep my eyes and ears focused on Him and not listening to the negativity in the world all around me.

Ralph Waldo Emerson once said, "The sun shines and warms and lights us and we have no curiosity to know why this is so; but we ask the reason of all evil, of pain, and hunger, and mosquitoes and silly people." I am quite content when things go my way, but little distractions can really get me side-tracked. It takes faith to stand strong through difficulties, trusting that God has prepared each day for me and promises to give me everything I need.

There is an inspiring quote by Soren Kierkegaard that says, "Faith is the highest passion in a human being. Many in every generation may not come that far, but none comes further." I want to be one in my generation that pursues faith - to have that passion and continually pray for greater faith. In the second and third chapters of Revelation, Jesus speaks seven times about "him who overcomes" and He promises rewards for the one who is "successful" in overcoming. First John 5:3-4 says "For this is what love for God is: to keep His commands. Now His commands are not a burden, because whatever has been born of God conquers the world. This is the victory that has conquered the world: our faith." With my faith I can conquer the world - I know that is true. How exciting! When I look at the lives of great people, I see their trust is in One greater. Faith is not easy, and it requires doubt in order to truly be faith. If there weren't doubt, faith would be more like "common sense". But faith is counter-intuitive - it requires seeing beyond the natural, trusting in Someone we cannot see. But faith is also the opposite of doubt, and the stronger your faith becomes, the weaker doubt will become. Trust Him and you will overcome!

"For I know the plans I have for you," declares the LORD, "plans to prosper you and not to harm you, plans to give you hope and a future" (Jeremiah 29:11)

Wide-Eyed Wonder

"Right at the crest, where Mount Olives begins its descent, the whole crowd of disciples burst into enthusiastic praise over all the mighty works they had witnessed: Blessed is He who comes, the King in God's name! All's well in heaven! Glory in the high places! Some Pharisees from the crowd told Him, "Teacher, get your disciples under control!" But He said, "If they kept quiet, the stones would do it for them, shouting praise." (Luke 19:37-40)

I often think of how we "ruin" some moments of our days by getting frustrated and bored with certain aspects of our lives. I recently took a vacation to a remote lake in Canada, and I enjoyed every minute of it (since I was on vacation). It hit me when the "locals" conversed about their annoying commute to town when they had to make a trip to pick something up. It was a four hour ride along a (rocky, two-track) beautifully wooded trail through the forest. Both entering and leaving, I held my camera close, optimistically hoping to spot a moose, eagle or bear and enjoying the beautiful lakes and horizons. And I did get the opportunity to capture a few pictures of bears and we saw some moose and eagles, as well as many other beautiful sights.

When we're young, we are so easily "entertained" by watching a butterfly or even a worm crawling along the ground. We should never lose that wonder. The beauty in the sunrise and sunset should never be taken for granted. I love the verse about the rocks crying out because it makes me realize I never want to take lightly God's creation and the majesty and splendor of what He has blessed us with. We disregard God's creativity and power when we lose interest in things around us - it is easy to do with repetition. But we need to jar ourselves awake and become curious once again. We love how exhilarated children become when they see things for the very first time. Imagine how pleased God is when we say "thank You" for all the little things He provides for us! Do not let yourself become desensitized by the monotony and distractions in life.

A quote from the book *Orthodoxy* by G. K. Chesterton says: "The child's cry for more is a quality of the very God who created them. It is possible that God says every morning, 'Do it again' to the sun; and every evening, 'Do it again' to the moon. It may not be automatic necessity that makes all daisies alike; it may be that God makes every daisy separately, but has never got tired of making them. It may be that He has the eternal appetite of infancy; for we have sinned and grown old, and our Father is younger than we. The repetition in Nature may not be a mere recurrence; it may be a theatrical *encore*."

Matthew 18:2-5 ~ For an answer Jesus called over a child, whom he stood in the middle of the room, and said, "I'm telling you, once and for all, that unless you return to square one and start over like children, you're not even going to get a look at the kingdom, let alone get in. Whoever becomes simple and elemental again, like this child, will rank high in God's kingdom. What's more, when you receive the childlike on my account, it's the same as receiving me.

Free to be me!

"But whoever catches a glimpse of the revealed counsel of God - the free life! - even out of the corner of his eye, and sticks with it, is no distracted scatterbrain but a man or woman of action. That person will find delight and affirmation in the action." (James 1:25)

One of the great challenges in life is where to draw the line – where do we place our boundaries? There is a lot of variation in the answer to that question from person to person, depending on their personality, life experiences, level of discipline while growing up and even birth order. We all love freedom, but we all view our freedom differently. I'm so grateful for the counsel of God. Galatians 5:1 says, "Christ has set us free to live a free life. So take your stand! Never again let anyone put a harness of slavery on you."

Because of the way we view things, many people think that doing whatever they want is freedom – and that usually means breaking the law. But in wrong-doing, we are actually walking in bondage. When we demand our own way and do things we know we shouldn't, we deceive ourselves, which leads to darkness. When our mind is darkened by bondage, we cannot see our way back to freedom. But perfect love – God's love - removes fear (bondage). One of the great benefits of freedom is the lack of condemnation, which is manifest in feelings of guilt and shame. When we recognize how much God loves us, bondage is removed from our life and we become truly free! That is why talking to Him daily, acknowledging Him in our life and searching out His plan for us is so important.

"God is love. When we take up permanent residence in a life of love, we live in God and God lives in us. This way, love has the run of the house, becomes at home and mature in us, so that we're free of worry on Judgment Day - our standing in the world is identical with Christ's. There is no room in love for fear. Well-formed love banishes fear. Since fear is crippling, a fearful life - fear of death, fear of judgment - is one not yet fully formed in love. We, though, are going to love - love and be loved. First we were loved, now we love. He loved us first." (1 John 4:17-19)

Many people believe that becoming a Christian limits the potential activities and opportunities that life offers – others say it's a license to do whatever you want. Here is what the bible says about freedom and rules: "Looking at it one way, you could say, 'Anything goes. Because of God's immense generosity and grace, we don't have to dissect and scrutinize every action to see if it will pass muster.' But the point is not to just get by. We want to live well, but our foremost efforts should be to help others live well.

With that as a base to work from, common sense can take you the rest of the way. Eat anything sold at the butcher shop, for instance; you don't have to run an "idolatry test" on every item. "The earth," after all, "is God's, and everything in it." That "everything" certainly includes the leg of lamb in the butcher shop. If a nonbeliever invites you to dinner and you feel like going, go ahead and enjoy yourself; eat everything placed before you. It would be both bad manners and bad spirituality to cross-examine your host on the ethical purity of each course as it is served. On the other hand, if he goes out of his way to tell you that this or that was sacrificed to god or goddess so-and-so, you should pass. Even though you may be indifferent as to where it came from, he isn't, and you don't want to send mixed messages to him about who you are worshiping.

But, except for these special cases, I'm not going to walk around on eggshells worrying about what small-minded people might say; I'm going to stride free and easy, knowing what our large-minded Master has already said. If I eat what is served to me, grateful to God for what is on the table, how can I worry about what someone will say? I thanked God for it and He blessed it!

So eat your meals heartily, not worrying about what others say about you - you're eating to God's glory, after all, not to please them. As a matter of fact, do everything that way, heartily and freely to God's glory. At the same time, don't be callous in your exercise of freedom, thoughtlessly stepping on the toes of those who aren't as free as you are. I try my best to be considerate of everyone's feelings in all these matters; I hope you will be, too." (I Corinthians 10:23-33)

The key theme in that passage is obedience; use common sense. Acts 10:15 says, "If God says it's OK, it's

OK." So the spirit of religion that some churches apply to add extra rules assume you cannot hear from God yourself (many people do not take the time to hear from God themselves). But if you have a relationship with God where you meet with Him every day, talking to Him, listening for His voice to speak to your heart and reading through the bible to know Him more, you can discern God's will and know right from wrong. Church is important for general guidance since we may become deceived from time to time, but our personal relationship with God should always supersede others' opinions. When Jesus died on the cross and the curtain in the temple was torn, we gained access to God. That is for our benefit so we can boldly approach the throne of grace to receive mercy and obtain favor from God. He will help us with every need when we seek Him.

"With that kind of hope to excite us, nothing holds us back. Unlike Moses, we have nothing to hide. Everything is out in the open with us. He wore a veil so the children of Israel wouldn't notice that the glory was fading away - and they didn't notice. They didn't notice it then and they don't notice it now, don't notice that there's nothing left behind that veil. Even today when the proclamations of that old, bankrupt government are read out, they can't see through it. Only Christ can get rid of the veil so they can see for themselves that there's nothing there. Whenever, though, they turn to face God as Moses did, God removes the veil and there they are - face-to-face! They suddenly recognize that God is a living, personal presence, not a piece of chiseled stone. And when God is personally present, a living Spirit, that old, constricting legislation is recognized as obsolete. We're free of it! All of us! Nothing between us and God, our faces shining with the brightness of His face. And so we are transfigured much like the Messiah, our lives gradually becoming brighter and more beautiful as God enters our lives and we become like Him." (2 Corinthians 3:12-18)

Knowing God leads to greater understanding and greater freedom in life. We do have to be careful about how we influence others, but we don't have to feel burdened or guilty any more. "But fortunately God doesn't grade us on our diet. We're neither commended when we clean our plate nor reprimanded when we just can't stomach it. But God does care when you use your freedom carelessly in a way that leads a fellow believer still vulnerable to those old associations to be thrown off track." (1 Corinthians 8:9)

Here are some more verses on how to live in freedom and enjoy life abundantly!

"All this is proceeding along lines planned all along by God and then executed in Christ Jesus. When we trust in Him, we're free to say whatever needs to be said, bold to go wherever we need to go. So don't let my present trouble on your behalf get you down. Be proud!" (Ephesians 3:12)

"Make the Master proud of you by being good citizens. Respect the authorities, whatever their level; they are God's emissaries for keeping order. It is God's will that by doing good, you might cure the ignorance of the fools who think you're a danger to society. Exercise your freedom by serving God, not by breaking the rules. Treat everyone you meet with dignity. Love your spiritual family. Revere God. Respect the government." (1 Peter 2:16)

"So let's agree to use all our energy in getting along with each other. Help others with encouraging words; don't drag them down by finding fault. You're certainly not going to permit an argument over what is served or not served at supper to wreck God's work among you, are you? I said it before and I'll say it again: All food is good, but it can turn bad if you use it badly, if you use it to trip others up and send them sprawling. When you sit down to a meal, your primary concern should not be to feed your own face but to share the life of Jesus. So be sensitive and courteous to the others who are eating. Don't eat or say or do things that might interfere with the free exchange of love." (Romans 14:19-21)

"With the arrival of Jesus, the Messiah, that fateful dilemma is resolved. Those who enter into Christ's being-here-for-us no longer have to live under a continuous, low-lying black cloud. A new power is in operation. The Spirit of life in Christ, like a strong wind, has magnificently cleared the air, freeing you from a fated lifetime of brutal tyranny at the hands of sin and death." (Romans 8:1-2)

Live free! And that's all I have to say about that.

Your Story

"He who believes in Me [who cleaves to and trusts in and relies on Me] as the Scripture has said, from his innermost being shall flow [continuously] springs and rivers of living water." (John 7:38)

Based on our actions, we earn a reputation and even leave behind a legacy after we are gone from this world. In John 12, we read an interesting story and easily see the differences in people based on how they lived: Martha enjoyed serving, Lazarus preferred to fellowship, Mary generously worshipped and Judas was offended. They were all in the same place, with Jesus, and each one chose their actions. None of them were forced to play a role they weren't comfortable with - just as each of us flows through our days and weeks, following our habits and lifestyles and choosing how we live and react to the world around us.

Our relationship with Jesus greatly affects our relationships with others and how others see us. When we make time and put forth effort in talking to our Heavenly Father and hearing from Him, others will know that we've been in His presence. His peace, love, joy, humility and mercy are uncommon in this world, and as they overflow from within us, others notice the difference! "But if we walk in the light, as He is in the light, we have {true} fellowship with one another" (1 John 1:7). When we really know Jesus, others will be drawn to Him through us. "We love because He first loved us" (1 John 4:19).

We were created for relationship - first with God, then with the people He places in our life. We learn about ourselves in relationships with others. And, as we learn how to handle situations in the diversity of other people, we learn more about the God who created us in His image. So we need to balance our time studying God's words to us in the bible and our time with other people. That way we can piece together how to best represent Him to those who might not otherwise know Him. The bible is filled with keys to understanding how to relate to other people. God maps out His path to repentance and restoration for us in the stories that make up the bible (history = His story).

Mary anointed Jesus for his day of burial and Jesus said "wherever the gospel is preached throughout the world, what she has done will also be told, in memory of her." So Mary is "famous" for her actions! We all know about the life of Judas and how his life ended because of his actions. Just as those people left behind their legacy, so too will we leave a story or remembrance that sums up our life here on earth. You have the ability to make that story whatever you will based on your actions today. We need to make every effort to know God and completely rely on Him for everything, to talk to Him about everything and everyone and make sure our behavior reflects the love of God - in the things we say and the things we do. Just as we want our friends to trust us, we know that God is pleased when we trust Him for the impossible. Apart from God, we can do nothing, but with God all things are possible.

Let's make each moment a memory that we are proud to leave behind - one that will draw others to the love of Christ and make their lives part of His story by our positive influence. Because of Jesus Christ, we have the authority and power to touch lives in an eternally significant way. We have been called a friend of God!

John 15:15 says, "No longer do I call you servants... but now I call you friends... for all things I have heard from My Father, I have shared with you." I love this verse because it proves that God created us, among many other reasons, to be a friend. Friends have fun together, laugh, share secrets, have common interests and communicate often! Some characteristics of true friends are loyalty, patience, forgiveness, honesty, equality. We treat our friends this way and we want to have the same response from our friends. Looks at your relationship with God and with others today and make sure your story will show others your first priority was God.

In Matthew 22:37-40, Jesus said, "'Love the Lord your God with all your passion and prayer and intelligence.' This is the most important, the first on any list. But there is a second to set alongside it: 'Love others as well as you love yourself.' These two commands are pegs; everything in God's Law and the Prophets hangs from them."

Trusting God's Friendship

"Show me Your ways, O Lord; teach me Your paths. Guide me in Your truth and faithfulness and teach me, for You are the God of my salvation; for You [You only and altogether] do I wait [expectantly] all the day long. Remember, O Lord, Your tender mercy and loving-kindness; for they have been ever from of old. All the paths of the Lord are mercy and steadfast love, even truth and faithfulness are they for those who keep His covenant and His testimonies. Who is the man who reverently fears and worships the Lord? Him shall He teach in the way that he should choose. He himself shall dwell at ease, and his offspring shall inherit the land. The secret [of the sweet, satisfying companionship] of the Lord have they who fear (revere and worship) Him, and He will show them His covenant and reveal to them its [deep, inner] meaning." (Psalm 25:4-6, 10, 12-14)

Recently, it seems like a lot of my prayers are unanswered. In reality, they are more like "optimistic wishes" – but I prefer to call them prayers of "great faith". And we know that without faith, it's impossible to please God. So surely He delights in us when we say prayers of "great faith"! For example, my prayer for a recent vacation trip to northern Ontario went something like this: "Lord, please let there be a miraculously late hatch for black flies this year and beyond normal temperatures for us this week." Prior to the trip I was talking to a friend of mine about our great expectations in life and how they sometimes lead to huge disappointments. After three days of snow and one with rain on our five-day fishing and camping vacation, I became a bit disheartened and began to really think about why God seems to "let us down" at times. I laugh now when I think about it. I was discouraged that I didn't see MORE moose on the trip, have warmer temperatures and catch the biggest pike ever seen! But I did give thanks that the black flies froze to death and I was grateful for the bear I was able to capture in photos, the moose bulls and eagles we saw, the surprise of morel mushrooms surrounding our camp site, the relaxing time I spent enjoying the scenery and reading, the opportunity to remain optimistic in camp with friends - and time well spent with my husband.

I realize now that I had started thinking about God as a "lucky rabbit's foot" instead of the sovereign "lover of my soul" that He is – and as I thought about it more, I realized that nobody enjoys spending time around spoiled children. From God's perspective, my requests probably aren't all that important in the big scheme of things. And if I received every petty little request, my personality wouldn't be as charming as it could be – spoiled kids whine and become weak-willed. But strength of character comes as we struggle through life's tougher experiences - and when we choose to be optimistic in the face of ugly circumstances. A great quote from Epictetus says "I am always content with what happens; for I know that what God chooses is better than what I choose." I am so thankful that I can trust God, hand the "reins of life" over to Him and know that I am in good hands!

Isaiah 30:15, 20-21 (AMP) For thus said the Lord God, the Holy One of Israel: In returning [to Me] and resting [in Me] you shall be saved; in quietness and in [trusting] confidence shall be your strength. And though the Lord gives you the bread of adversity and the water of affliction, yet your Teacher will not hide Himself any more, but your eyes will constantly behold your Teacher. And your ears will hear a word behind you, saying, "This is the way; walk in it, when you turn to the right hand and when you turn to the left."

The Race

"What we have is one body with many parts, each its proper size and in its proper place. No part is important on its own." (I Corinthians 12:20)

At times, life seems like a sprint and at others I feel like those people looked in the Beijing Olympics marathon, barely making each foot step in front of the other – and feeling like dropping out. But more recently I've decided that life within the body of Christ is more similar to a relay. When things get too tough to handle by ourselves, we can pass the baton to a brother or sister, and they will carry on for us until we are restored and strengthened again.

Romans 12:4-6 says "… we are like the various parts of a human body. Each part gets its meaning from the body as a whole, not the other way around." (Think about that! We are sometimes tempted to see how our gift shapes the body we're in – but that's the wrong perspective!) "The body we're talking about is Christ's body of chosen people. Each of us finds our meaning and function as a part of His body. But as a chopped-off finger or cut-off toe we wouldn't amount to much, would we? So since we find ourselves fashioned into all these excellently formed and marvelously functioning parts in Christ's body, let's just go ahead and be what we were made to be, without enviously or pridefully comparing ourselves with each other, or trying to be something we aren't."

In order to run in a relay race together, each team member needs the other. Likewise, in order to have harmony in a band, each band member needs the other band members. We need our family members within the body of Christ to fulfill our Heavenly Father's purpose for us – to bring glory to His name and to bring more people into His kingdom! We don't criticize another's abilities or compete with each other, but we work together, each one completing the task we're uniquely qualified for. I love authentic Mexican cuisine, but I never sit around munching on cilantro leaves. It takes all the ingredients, carefully measured, to make a recipe taste just right. God has done all the "measuring" already! All we have to do is apply ourselves where He has gifted us. We should never doubt that God has gifted each and every single one of us - and we should never compare our gifts with others'. We're in this thing together, and it requires each one of us to do our part.

Colossians 3:23 ~ In all the work you are doing, work the best you can. Work as if you were doing it for the Lord, not for people.

God's Plan for Success

"The kingdom of heaven is like a grain of mustard seed that a man took and sowed in his field. It is the smallest of all seeds, but when it has grown it is larger than all the garden plants and becomes a tree, so that the birds of the air come and make nests in its branches." (Matthew 13:31-32)

This parable that Jesus shared seems simple enough to be shared with children, and yet holds enough promise and hope to glean long beyond our childhood. When we think of heaven, many times we think of our future – eternity. But the kingdom of heaven is here, now. It is good to reflect on what we expect in this life, how we live throughout each day, the words we speak and what kind of seeds we might be sowing – and realize we are continually planting something that will yield its harvest at some point further down the road of life. "Sow for yourselves righteousness, reap the fruit of unfailing love, and break up your unplowed ground; for it is time to seek the Lord, until He comes and showers righteousness on you." (Hosea 10:12) As children of God, we are encouraged to live in obedience to God's Word – and by faith we trust He is directing us along this road, and we are storing up treasure in heaven. God loves journeys, as we can see from many stories in the bible: from darkness into light, from blindness to vision, from the familiar to the unexpected, from thirst to provision and from slavery in Egypt to freedom in the Promised Land, overflowing with abundance. When we make the determination to follow God's plan for our life, we should anticipate great things! We have stepped out of the kingdom of this world and into the kingdom of heaven, by faith.

We need to encourage others to seek Him for everything. In our weakness, His strength is made perfect! Ask Him to open your eyes to see things you never believed were possible. His storehouse is unending – we can never ask for anything too difficult for God to do, and nothing we ask is insignificant because He loves us more than we can imagine. He already has an answer to our biggest problems, but He asks us to relate it to Him in our own words – and in the process we understand ourselves more - and learn more about God and His love for us. When we seek God's heart and His purpose, He gives us keys to unlock greater blessings for this adventure. Life in God's kingdom requires talking to Him and trusting Him completely, but once we've stepped out in faith God does all the work! He who did not spare His own Son, but delivered Him up for us all, how shall He not with Him also freely give us all things? (Romans 8:32)

Never compare your past or your current circumstances to where you think you can go. When you compare a kernel of corn to a mustard seed, it becomes obvious that the size of the final product is never evident by the size of the seed. There are many factors that will cause different growth rates. The amount of sun or water that a seed is exposed to can help or hinder its growth. In the same way, our obedience and level of faith can help "grow" the seeds we've planted. So we should never consider "small beginnings" (Zech 4:10) because we do not know God's plan for the future! Everyday we see the perfection and excellence He has created to bless us in the sunrise, sunset and the beauty of the trees and animals. When we struggle in life, it is always refreshing to focus on His handiwork. God created the heavens and the earth in seven days. God raised Jesus from the dead in three days – nothing is too difficult for Him! Everything is subject to change in a moment with God's help. He can cause a meager beginning to become a wonderful work beyond our imagination – trust Him!

And we pray this in order that you may live a life worthy of the Lord and may please Him in every way: bearing fruit in every good work, growing in the knowledge of God, being strengthened with all power according to His glorious might so that you may have great endurance and patience, and joyfully giving thanks to the Father, who has qualified you to share in the inheritance of the saints in the kingdom of light. (Colossians 1:10-12)

Grace, Love and Worship Defined

"A time will come, however, indeed it is already here, when the true (genuine) worshipers will worship the Father in spirit and in truth (reality); for the Father is seeking just such people as these as His worshipers." (John 4:23)

I love the story about the woman who anointed Jesus' feet with her tears and perfume – and received forgiveness because of her faith, gratitude and love. To me, that is the purest definition of "true worship"… an act of faith that expresses absolute devotion and unconditional love for Jesus, focusing on Him alone. This woman's actions were sincere – she did not have ulterior motives. Devotion, loyalty, and unselfish love are very rare qualities between friends today.

We do not risk exposing ourselves to ridicule in wholehearted vulnerability and raw emotion like that woman did. Her reputation as a sinner was well known among those attending the meal with Jesus. But she dismissed her concern for their approval of her actions and she set aside any pride while humbly focusing her affection upon Jesus. I wonder if we are honest enough with ourselves to even know the depth of concern this woman felt, without consideration of what others might think of us today.

Her joy and appreciation for the love and acceptance she received from Jesus is remarkable. Her attitude is one of total surrender and trust. Do we portray that level of trust toward God in our actions?

The parable that Jesus shares to communicate what is really going on is simple and to the point: there are two people indebted to a creditor. One debt is ten times the debt of the other's, but the creditor completely forgives both debts – not because either deserves it, but based on grace alone. Which debtor is more appreciative of the grace extended to him? The Pharisee to whom the question is directed replies correctly: the one with the greater debt is more grateful for having that debt cancelled.

"The one who has been forgiven much, loves much." It is humbling to think about how undeserving we are of God's goodness toward us. In appreciation we respond to His love and mercy, and in return we receive His favor all the more. There is nothing we can do to repay God for all He has done for us – and when we realize how far we are from His holiness and How richly He lavishes His love upon us, we should be overwhelmed with joy and appreciation, much like this woman. Our lives should be spent focusing, worshipping and adoring our King! Wherever we are in life, God's message remains the same – He will respond when we turn to Him! And when we live for God, we become messengers of His love to those who do not yet know Him. God's love can completely reverse the effects of sin whenever someone seeks God's forgiveness in humility. In response to His mercy, forgiveness, grace and compassion we are compelled to love Him and live for His glory!

Luke 7:47 ~ "I tell you, her sins - and they are many - have been forgiven, so she has shown me much love. But a person who is forgiven little shows only little love."

Greater Vision

"I know that You can do all things, and that no thought or purpose of Yours can be restrained or thwarted." (Job 42:2)

No matter what happens in life, it is so comforting to remember that God is still on His throne, in control of all things. I am so thankful that He is always sovereign! Last week I had some plans made and didn't realize I'd forgotten to enter an appointment into my calendar. Unforeseen events caused all my plans to change, and the activities that ultimately came to pass resulted in some family wounds being healed in an unbelievable way. I never would have been able to experience that if I had organized my calendar according to "priorities" in my own mind. God had other plans, and everything worked out perfectly – beyond that, even! It is so neat to realize how God causes us to see certain things and blinds us from seeing other things to make His purposes prevail. I am grateful that He understands how limited my vision can be at times and works around my shortcomings to bless me and those I love.

I pray that God, the source of hope, will fill you completely with joy and peace because you trust in Him. Then you will overflow with confident hope through the power of the Holy Spirit. ~Rom 15:13

God knows what we need before we do - and He sees "the big picture" – from beginning to end. So let's continue to put our trust in Him for all things! Many times, to increase my faith and vision, and see things from God's perspective, I find it helpful to write things down as they happen and record my prayer requests on a daily basis. Then, when my prayers are answered, it is so amazing to look at the way God answered those prayers, compared to my limited ideas that I had beforehand. His ways are so much higher than my ways! It is humbling to think about, but also results in overwhelming appreciation for how God moves "behind the scenes" to take care of every detail in our lives!

For God's foolishness is wiser than human wisdom, and God's weakness is stronger than human strength. (I Cor 1:25)

Full Access to Opportunities

"By entering through faith into what God has always wanted to do for us - set us right with Him, make us fit for Him - we have it all together with God because of our Master Jesus. And that's not all: We throw open our doors to God and discover at the same moment that He has already thrown open His door to us. We find ourselves standing where we always hoped we might stand - out in the wide open spaces of God's grace and glory, standing tall and shouting praise." (Rom 5:1-2)

As Christians we have the opportunity to help people because of our position in Christ. Since we are children of God we have access to unlimited power when we put our faith in action. Through our relationship with our Heavenly Father, we can help people by introducing them to Jesus and He can remove their debts completely, if they receive Him as their Savior. In Luke 16, a story is told of a wise steward: (Lk 16:1-12) Jesus told his disciples: "There was a rich man whose manager was accused of wasting his possessions. So he called him in and asked him, 'What is this I hear about you? Give an account of your management, because you cannot be manager any longer.'

"The manager said to himself, 'What shall I do now? My master is taking away my job. I'm not strong enough to dig, and I'm ashamed to beg - I know what I'll do so that, when I lose my job here, people will welcome me into their houses.' "So he called in each one of his master's debtors. He asked the first, 'How much do you owe my master?' "'Eight hundred gallons of olive oil,' he replied. "The manager told him, 'Take your bill, sit down quickly, and make it four hundred.' "Then he asked the second, 'And how much do you owe?' 'A thousand bushels of wheat,' he replied. "He told him, 'Take your bill and make it eight hundred.'

"The master commended the dishonest manager because he had acted shrewdly. For the people of this world are more shrewd in dealing with their own kind than are the people of the light. I tell you, use worldly wealth to gain friends for yourselves, so that when it is gone, you will be welcomed into eternal dwellings.

"Whoever can be trusted with very little can also be trusted with much, and whoever is dishonest with very little will also be dishonest with much. So if you have not been trustworthy in handling worldly wealth, who will trust you with true riches? And if you have not been trustworthy with someone else's property, who will give you property of your own?

The manager took advantage of his position and helped the people who were indebted to his master. How much more should we be providing the solution for others' difficulties – Jesus is the answer to every problem.

And we hold the keys to the kingdom of God within us when we should be freely offering the truth to those in our sphere of influence. Ephesians 2:1-10 says, "It wasn't so long ago that you were mired in that old stagnant life of sin. You let the world, which doesn't know the first thing about living, tell you how to live. You filled your lungs with polluted unbelief, and then exhaled disobedience. We all did it, all of us doing what we felt like doing, when we felt like doing it, all of us in the same boat. It's a wonder God didn't lose his temper and do away with the whole lot of us. Instead, immense in mercy and with an incredible love, He embraced us. He took our sin-dead lives and made us alive in Christ. He did all this on his own, with no help from us! Then He picked us up and set us down in highest heaven in company with Jesus, our Messiah.

Now God has us where He wants us, with all the time in this world and the next to shower grace and kindness upon us in Christ Jesus. Saving is all His idea, and all His work. All we do is trust Him enough to let Him do it. It's God's gift from start to finish! We don't play the major role. If we did, we'd probably go around bragging that we'd done the whole thing! No, we neither make nor save ourselves. God does both the making and saving. He creates each of us by Christ Jesus to join Him in the work He does, the good work He has gotten ready for us to do, work we had better be doing."

This is not only for our advantage, but for the benefit of those around us. We are to touch eternal souls for good – to impact people the way Jesus would. We are responsible to follow through, in obedience to God's word, and be good stewards (managers) of what He has given us and the purposes He has commanded us to complete. By faith, we act as vessels for God's power to flow through and touch eternal souls.

II Peter 1:3-8 says, "Everything that goes into a life of pleasing God has been miraculously given to us by getting to know, personally and intimately, the One who invited us to God. The best invitation we ever received! We were also given absolutely terrific promises to pass on to you - your tickets to participation in the life of God after you turned your back on a world corrupted by lust. So don't lose a minute in building on what you've been given, complementing your basic faith with good character, spiritual understanding, alert discipline, passionate patience, reverent wonder, warm friendliness, and generous love, each dimension fitting into and developing the others. With these qualities active and growing in your lives, no grass will grow under your feet; no day will pass without its reward as you mature in your experience of our Master Jesus. Without these qualities you can't see what's right before you, oblivious that your old sinful life has been wiped off the books."

More than Conquerors

"I had heard rumors about You, but now my eyes have seen You." (Job 42:5)

I think I missed my calling in life... I love being outside and I love playing in the dirt. As kids, my brother and I were so focused on having fun outside we didn't even realize how filthy we were until we thought about going in the house. Many times we'd sneak down to the basement where the laundry was and slip on some clean clothes before Mom spotted us. So for me, a career in archaeology seems like the most fascinating job, and fun life, I can imagine. Just reading about the archaeological finds gives me goose bumps! It's a strange feeling when I sense the connection between my brain and my heart - faith meeting with physical evidence that supports what I believe. Imagine finding a 30' x 8' boat, that would hold approximately 15 passengers found in 1986 near Tiberias, Israel, that would be like the boats Jesus' disciples used in crossing the Sea of Galilee. Carbon 14 dating places the boat between 120 BC and AD 40. That could be the very boat we read about in the bible! It might seem insignificant to many, but it makes my imagination go wild! They say seeing is believing, but when you already believe something and then see evidence confirming what you believe in, it is far more exciting than just seeing and then believing!

When I think about Job's life, it is encouraging to

see what he went through and how he maintained his devotion to God. We are called to persevere through trials, knowing God is near even when we do not feel His presence. (Romans 5:3-5 says "...we also rejoice in our afflictions, because we know that affliction produces endurance, endurance produces proven character, and proven character produces hope. This hope does not disappoint, because God's love has been poured out in our hearts through the Holy Spirit who was given to us.") When we see Him face to face, we will know why we had to endure tough situations in our life on earth – and I'm sure they will seem small then! They are not without purpose, and by faith we need to hold on and trust our Heavenly Father. James 1:2-4 says "Consider it pure joy, my brothers, whenever you face trials of many kinds, because you know that the testing of your faith develops perseverance. Perseverance must finish its work so that you may be mature and complete, not lacking anything."

We know that every good and perfect gift comes from God. The life we live on earth is meant to prepare us for what is ahead. Whenever we face difficulties, we need to thank God that He is sovereign, He sees our predicament and He will be faithful to strengthen us. Psalm 37:23-25 says, "If the LORD delights in a man's way, He makes his steps firm; though he stumble, he will not fall, for the LORD upholds him with His hand. I was young and now I am old, yet I have never seen the righteous forsaken or their children begging bread." We live each day for God's glory, trusting He will bring about good when we are obedient to Him. When Job learned to trust in God's sufficiency instead of his own wealth and let go of his fear, knowing God's goodness, he received his greatest blessing. We need to trust that situations we face are meant to draw us closer to God and give us a greater understanding of how He wants us to depend on Him for everything. Job 42:10, 12 ~ "After Job had prayed for his friends, the Lord restored his prosperity and doubled his previous possessions. So the Lord blessed the latter part of Job's life more than the earlier..." Similarly, Paul writes: "I consider that our present sufferings are not worth comparing with the glory that will be revealed in us." (Rom 8:18) and "For God's foolishness is wiser than human wisdom, and God's weakness is stronger than human strength." (I Corinthians 1:25)

Consider these encouraging words from Paul in Rom 8:28-39: "And we know that in all things God works for the good of those who love Him, who have been called according to His purpose... What, then, shall we say in response to this? If God is for us, who can be against us? He who did not spare His own Son, but gave Him up for us all — how will He not also, along with Him, graciously give us all things? Who will bring any charge against those whom God has chosen? It is God who justifies. Who is he that condemns? Christ Jesus, who died — more than that, who was raised to life — is at the right hand of God and is also interceding for us. Who shall separate us from the love of Christ? Shall trouble or hardship or persecution or famine or nakedness or danger or sword?

As it is written: 'For your sake we face death all day long; we are considered as sheep to be slaughtered.' <u>No, in all these things we are more than conquerors through Him who loved us</u>. For I am convinced that neither death nor life, neither angels nor demons, neither the present nor the future, nor any powers, neither height nor depth, nor anything else in all creation, will be able to separate us from the love of God that is in Christ Jesus our Lord."

Living in Freedom and Victory

"Now the Lord is the Spirit and where the Spirit of the Lord is, there is liberty (freedom). And all of us, as with unveiled face, [because we] continued to behold [in the Word of God] as in a mirror the glory of the Lord, are constantly being transfigured into His very own image in ever-increasing splendor and from one degree of glory to another; [for this comes] from the Lord [Who is] the Spirit." (II Cor 3:17-18)

Every one of us has days when we stumble and lose a battle against our flesh; when our anger, pride, fear or lust is brought to the surface and we do what we do not want to do (Rom 7:16). When our heart is sincere and we seek forgiveness, fully intending to turn away from that behavior, God's forgiveness is there for us.

Since I John 1:9 tells us God is faithful to forgive us, we know we are given a clean slate – and will continue to be given a clean slate whenever we ask for His forgiveness and begin to obey Him. Let's stop walking through life feeling condemned. Romans 8:1 tells us there is no condemnation for those who are in Christ. We are children of God in the process of being conformed into the likeness of Jesus. As we grow and mature, God's Spirit within us guarantees our victory! Let's walk in that victory! With a thankful heart, express to God your love and gratitude to Him as you greet Him each morning. In our weaknesses, His strength is made perfect – let's walk in that strength today! When we draw near to God, He promises to draw near to us. Give Him all you have and watch Him work in your life in extraordinary ways! He wants to bless you more than you know – and He wants us to live victoriously, walking in His supernatural strength each day.

"He shall be like a tree Planted by the rivers of water, That brings forth its fruit in its season, Whose leaf also shall not wither; And whatever he does shall prosper." - Ps 1:3

Seeking God's Favor

"Laboring together [as God's fellow workers] with Him then, we beg of you not to receive the grace of God in vain [that merciful kindness by which God exerts His holy influence on souls and turns them to Christ, keeping and strengthening them - do not receive it to no purpose]. For He says, 'In the time of favor (of an assured welcome) I have listened to and heeded your call, and I have helped you on the day of deliverance (the day of salvation). Behold, now is truly the time for a gracious welcome and acceptance [of you from God]; behold, now is the day of salvation!'" (II Cor. 6:1-2)

The other day I was wondering why I don't pray more often about things that matter to me. When I put forth the effort to pray about every little detail I may face and give all those concerns to God, requesting His help, His favor and His perfect will in situations, I am amazed at His faithfulness and love toward me – "Oh, how He loves us"! (That's an awesome song, by the way, from the David Crowder Band.) I think we are fearful many times, but fail to admit it to ourselves, much less admit that to God. In our minds, we think we can hide from God – but our life is wide open right before Him, like a book. He sees everything about us, like looking through a microscope, but even better. Why do we wait so long to request His assistance sometimes? It might be that we realize our motives aren't pure, so we think we have to

make things happen on our own. How futile to even try –
we're producing wood, hay and stubble – what's the point?
The more I make myself think about God throughout the
day, and His unconditional love for me, the freer I feel!
There is so much liberty when we consider all that God
wants to do in and through us.

When we run into "people problems" the same is
true – consider others' needs as more important than your
own and realize the battle is not against flesh and blood.
The enemy of our soul wants to separate us from loved
ones – but people are in our life for a reason. God uses
them to change us… and there is a time and a season for
everything under the sun. Isaiah 1:18-20 (MSG) says:
"'Come. Sit down. Let's argue this out.' This is God's
Message: 'If your sins are blood-red, they'll be snow-
white. If they're red like crimson, they'll be like wool. If
you'll willingly obey, you'll feast like kings. But if you're
willful and stubborn, you'll die like dogs.' That's right.
God says so."

If we need to "reason with God", surely we will need
to reason with one another from time to time. So, let's
keep short accounts with one another, reason together and
be honest with one another. And more importantly, let's
be transparent before God. He can take care of anything,
especially relationships! First Peter 3:18 says "If with
heart and soul you're doing good, do you think you can
be stopped? Even if you suffer for it, you're still better
off. Don't give the opposition a second thought. Through
thick and thin, keep your hearts at attention, in adoration

before Christ, your Master. Be ready to speak up and tell anyone who asks why you're living the way you are, and always with the utmost courtesy. Keep a clear conscience before God so that when people throw mud at you, none of it will stick. They'll end up realizing that they're the ones who need a bath." A favorite pastor of mine once said, "Don't wrestle with the pigs; you'll both get dirty and the pig likes it!" In other words, walk away. It's not worth the effort – cast it over to God and He'll deal with the other person. When you look at the life of Jesus, He struggled with people throughout His days on earth, and He was the Son of God. How much more will we struggle, then, as we learn to be more like Christ? But we must remember to desire God's approval more than man's. Then we will have the favor of God - and that's all we need!

True Freedom

"Anyone who listens to the Word but does not do what it says is like a man who looks at his face in a mirror and, after looking at himself, goes away and immediately forgets what he looks like. But the man who looks intently into the perfect law that gives freedom, and continues to do this, not forgetting what he has heard, but doing it – he will be blessed in what he does." (James 1:23-25)

I read about an assignment given to a group of graduate students in seminary asked "Which person has the most freedom? The answers to choose from were: A - the person that is not able to sin, B - the person that is able to sin and able to not sin, or C - the person who is not able not to sin." The graduate students picked B – a person who is able to sin and able to not sin. However, they began to think about the disturbing question after picking their answer: who has more freedom than God? God is not able to sin. Our understanding of "freedom" is flawed; freedom is not necessarily about having choices.

True freedom is the ability to function according to God's design. Many people think Christians limit themselves by only doing what God tells them to; we must understand that we are at our optimum performance when we are doing what we were designed to do by the omniscient Creator of all things. Sin of any kind is a serious defect available to humans, who, in pursuit of sin, become a perverted form of God's original intent. All sin, whether or not anyone ever finds out about it, will lead to death and destruction.

A scripture often quoted out of context is "The truth shall make you free." That is a conditional statement based on the preceding verse: "To the Jews who had believed him, Jesus said, 'If you hold to my teaching, you are really my disciples. *Then* you will know the truth, and the truth will set you free.'" (John 8:31-32) When we purpose in our heart to become a disciple of Jesus Christ and wholeheartedly obey His commands, we find true freedom. We do not look at God's commands as ways to deprive us; instead, we understand our call to freedom in Christ. As a result, we are compelled to seek righteousness for ourselves and driven to lead the lost to a relationship with our Heavenly Father so they can become what He intended and be truly free.

From his sermon on the first Thanksgiving Day, after the war for independence in the US, John Witherspoon declared, "A republic once equally poised must either preserve its virtue or lose its liberty." (Francis Schaeffer, *A Christian Manifesto*, 33.)

Chapter Two – LOVE

Growing Your Knowing
Expands Your Love

"I will pursue Your commands, for You expand my understanding." (Psalm 119:32)

When we really pursue God, He increases our understanding. Proverbs 1:7 (CEV) says, "Respect and obey the Lord! This is the beginning of knowledge."

There is no one who compares with the wisdom of our Heavenly Father. God created everything we see and by His wisdom, He gave order to the world we live in - including the intricate details going on within us to sustain life. The deeper you study the human body, the more you will believe in the wisdom of our Creator! Through wisdom, God provided diverse creatures - and every human being He made possesses a unique personality. (We can easily see this since everyone has an opinion, and they all vary!) God created us to be different because He loves diversity. Often, we see different "religions" try to forces us to believe we all need to act the same. Enjoy the freedom of being who God created you to be!

The enemy of our soul is the source of confusion, but God can use confusion for His purposes (see Genesis 11:1-9). When we look at a map, we see that the Israelites could have left Egypt and reached Canaan in 5-6 weeks' time. Instead, God led them through the wilderness for 40 years! The Israelites plan was to leave "point A" and reach "point B" – but God's plans were higher (they always are). His desire was for His people to see Him and to know Him. He wanted to shape His people, to teach them, and to set an example for the rest of the world through them. When we read the Old Testament today, we can see how the stories of their lives bring glory to God. Many people in that day heard of the Israelites' victories and feared God as a result. Numerous "ripple effects" from the actions of God's people touched others outside the Israelite camp and changed the lives of those people forever. That is still God's plan for His people – for us: "The Christian life rooted in the secret place where God meets and walks and talks with His own grows into such a testimony of Divine power that all men will feel its influence and be touched by the warmth of its love." (E. M. Bounds)

One thing about maturity is that you can't "fake it"… nobody knows how to act mature – we must grow to become mature. In the same way, as we grow closer to God we become more like Him. We can't act "godly" until He leads us through our wilderness – which contains the experiences we need to learn about God so we can be more like Him. We almost always want to get from point A to point B the quickest way possible, but that isn't always God's plan – in fact, it seems like that's never God's plan. The trials and tests we face are for our own benefit – and the more uncomfortable we are, the more quickly we grow! Each of us has a unique "wilderness" to travel through before we get to the destination God has purposed for us. And in that wilderness, God leads us to learn to love one another the way He loves us. When we obey Him, He is faithful to increase our compassion for other people.

I recently read The Shack, and this discussion between Mack and Sarayu about Mack's children made me stop and think: ""…but even when they act badly, they are still my son or my daughter… and they will be forever. What they do might affect my pride, but not my love for them." [Sarayu] sat back, beaming. "You are wise in the ways of real love, Mackenzie. So many people believe that it is love that grows, but it is the knowing that grows and love simply expands to contain it. Love is just the skin of knowing."

God has a funny way of working in us. Once we begin to know and love the law of the Lord, we desire to know it more, and love it better. And often, the same is true with people – the more we really know them, the more we can understand their perspective and grow to love them. God, by His Spirit, enlarges the hearts of His people when He gives them wisdom. The disciple of Jesus prays to be set free from sin, and the knowledge of Him who loves us perfectly causes us to overlook offenses and love others with that same love. Follow Him through the wilderness and you will never be disappointed – He is forever faithful, completely compassionate and a steadfast refuge. Trust Him, pursue Him and grow in Him.

Psalm 119:26-40 says, "When I told you my troubles, You answered my prayers. Now teach me Your laws. Help me to understand Your teachings, and I will think about Your marvelous deeds. I am overcome with sorrow. Encourage me, as You have promised to do. Keep me from being deceitful, and be kind enough to teach me Your Law. I am determined to be faithful and to respect Your laws. I follow Your rules, LORD. Don't let me be ashamed. I am eager to learn all that You want me to do; help me to understand more and more. Point out Your rules to me, and I won't disobey even one of them. Help me to understand Your Law; I promise to obey it with all my heart. Direct me by Your commands! I love to do what You say. Make me want to obey You, rather than to be rich. Take away my foolish desires, and let me find life by walking with You. I am Your servant! Do for me what You promised to those who worship You. Your wonderful teachings protect me from the insults that I hate so much. I long for Your teachings. Be true to Yourself and let me live."

The Lover's Life

"So this is my prayer: that your love will flourish and that you will not only love much but well. Learn to love appropriately. You need to use your head and test your feelings so that your love is sincere and intelligent, not sentimental gush. Live a lover's life, circumspect and exemplary, a life Jesus will be proud of: bountiful in fruits from the soul, making Jesus Christ attractive to all, getting everyone involved in the glory and praise of God." (Philippians 1:9-11)

When I find myself considering what to do to make my life worthwhile, I feel overwhelmed. I need to be reminded from time to time that Jesus said "Come to Me, all you who are weary and burdened, and I will give you rest. Take My yoke upon you and learn from Me, for I am gentle and humble in heart, and you will find rest for your souls. For My yoke is easy and My burden is light."

The bible tells us over and over again that God is in control of everything, that He cares about every detail of our life and that His purposes will prevail: In Isaiah 55:8-11, the Lord says, "My thoughts are not like your thoughts. Your ways are not like My ways. Just as the heavens are higher than the earth, so are My ways higher than your ways and My thoughts higher than your thoughts. Rain and snow fall from the sky and don't return without watering the ground. They cause the plants to sprout and grow, making seeds for the farmer and bread for the people. The same thing is true of the words I speak. They will not return to Me empty. They make the things happen that I want to happen, and they succeed in doing what I send them to do."

When I look over my life and count all the times that God intervened to bring about real change and turn things around for me for good, I am amazed that I ever doubt Him or that I ever try to do things my way.

When we are obedient, God places us in favorable places. He gives us the advantage and works things out in such a way that we could never have dreamed was possible, because He sees the big picture. We need to see obstacles the way God sees them and we need to see other people the way God sees them. Life will be so much easier when we let go and trust Him completely for everything. Jeremiah 10:23-24 ~ "O Lord, I know that [the determination of] the way of a man is not in himself; it is not in man [even in a strong man or in a man at his best] to direct his [own] steps. O Lord, correct, instruct, and chastise me, but with judgment and in just measure- -not in Your anger, lest You diminish me and bring me to nothing."

Job 5:8-12 says, "But if I were you, I would call on God and bring my problem before Him. God does wonders that cannot be understood; He does so many miracles they cannot be counted. He gives rain to the earth and sends water on the fields. He makes the humble person important and lifts the sad to places of safety. He ruins the plans of those who trick others so they have no success."

It is so comforting to know that God will bring justice to our world in His timing. The plans of the ones who trick others will not be successful in the long run! We need to pray for God to bring justice, even when we don't see what others might be trying to do around us. He sees everything that goes on, including the motives of people's hearts. Trust Him!

Isaiah 40:28-31 says, "Surely you know. Surely you have heard. The LORD is the God who lives forever, who created all the world. He does not become tired or need to rest. No one can understand how great His wisdom is. He gives strength to those who are tired and more power to those who are weak. Even children become tired and need to rest, and young people trip and fall. But the people who trust the LORD will become strong again. They will rise up as an eagle in the sky; they will run and not need rest; they will walk and not become tired."

The Power of Love

"As the rain and the snow come down from heaven and do not return to it without watering the earth and making it bud and flourish, so that it yields seed for the sower and bread for the eater, so is My Word that goes out from My mouth: It will not return to Me empty, but will accomplish what I desire and achieve the purpose for which I sent it." (Isaiah 55:10-11)

The rain and snow fall on the earth causing growth in the grass, trees and flowers, but in the later winter to early spring the snow lies on the surface before the frost is driven out of the ground. So it is with us, when we harbor bitterness, unforgiveness and other characteristics of our "old nature". God's Word, sent to make us flourish and grow cannot benefit us until the old nature is driven out of us by God's love and our obedience.

The bible says that perfect love drives out fear. When we are without fear, we can accomplish a lot! And when we project the love of God out toward others, a lot of great relationships can "flourish" and we end up helping others more than we know.

God's love is an unconditional love – we need to share that with others. Nothing is as powerful as love! Sitting on the surface, the melting snow drowns any potentially new growth that might come out of the ground. Once the frost is gone, however, the water can penetrate the surface of the earth to nourish new growth. In the same way, once we remove our old, carnal nature – those things that hinder growth – layer by layer, the Word of God is able to penetrate deeper into our being to cause us to grow. As we grow, we influence others around us to grow as well. Soak in God's perfect love and pray that His love will flow through you into the love of others. Then sit back and enjoy watching the growth!

Stepping Up

"This is love for God: to obey His commands. And His commands are not burdensome, for everyone born of God overcomes the world. This is the victory that has overcome the world, even our faith. Who is it that overcomes the world? Only he who believes that Jesus is the Son of God." (I John 5:3-5)

Sometimes we think we need to step into the world to understand the worldly people and reach them. The dross we acquire by walking that road clouds our vision for what God would have us do. Like a polluted river, we become of no use whatsoever. Stepping closer to Him will allow you to see clearly what to say and do. We need to continually set our standards a little higher.

When you know Him like you know your closest friend, you'll know His will; you will recognize His voice among a thousand other opinions. He will lead you above and beyond anything you could ever imagine for your life. He will shake your world and get your attention as you take that first step of faith and obey Him; He will restore you.

The enemy takes away, but God multiplies! He will not only be your provision, but He will give you abundant life! He longs to take us to a higher place. Set your standard higher and don't be afraid to ask Him for great things - He has so much in store for us.

Challenge yourself to read and obey His words to you

in the bible, and keep your focus on Him. Make prayer time a delightful time – the best part of your day. Meet Him in that secret place where He can change you. He longs to know you more and we always need to know Him more – to become more like Him!

He will cause our relationships to flourish when we delight in our relationship with Him above everything else. The enemy would have you slowed down by distraction, but God accelerates! God's Holy Spirit can move so quickly in the lives of those around us as we lift them up in prayer.

Continually step it up a notch throughout your journey in life, challenging yourself to get closer to the Lord, becoming more like Jesus, loving others and showing compassion to each one you meet. Never lose heart – people will disappoint us, but God never will. When we challenge ourselves to obey Him, despite how we feel, we walk in His light and receive blessings from Him for obeying. This is what it means to work out our salvation - to become the person God created us to be: an overcomer!

Matthew 5:43-47 says, "You're familiar with the old written law, 'Love your friend' and its unwritten companion, 'Hate your enemy.' I'm challenging that. I'm telling you to love your enemies. Let them bring out the best in you, not the worst. When someone gives you a hard time, respond with the energies of prayer, for then you are working out of your true selves, your God-created selves. This is what God does. He gives his best - the sun to warm and the rain to nourish - to everyone, regardless: the good and bad, the nice and nasty. If all you do is love the lovable, do you expect a bonus? Anybody can do that. If you simply say hello to those who greet you, do you expect a medal? Any run-of-the-mill sinner does that."

A Spacious and Free Life

"Those who think they can do it on their own end up obsessed with measuring their own moral muscle but never get around to exercising it in real life. Those who trust God's action in them find that God's Spirit is in them - living and breathing God! Obsession with self in these matters is a dead end; attention to God leads us out into the open, into a spacious, free life. Focusing on the self is the opposite of focusing on God. Anyone completely absorbed in self ignores God, ends up thinking more about self than God. That person ignores who God is and what He is doing. And God isn't pleased at being ignored." (Romans 8:5-8)

I am amazed at how easily distracted I am! I never noticed it much before, especially in comparison with other people. But avoiding the trap of comparing myself with others, and looking directly at my ability to make time to focus on God reveals how quickly I get side-tracked. As I attempt to ensure that Jesus is still my "first love", I am repeatedly frustrated at the little things that flit through my thoughts, completely diverting my attention away from what's really important. These little whims are like the gods that the Israelites found themselves continually tempted to build up.

During the first week of the New Year, I made a resolution to review my "original" resolutions on a monthly basis in order to measure my progress (or lack thereof) and maintain my course. As the year unfolds, I like to improve my plans to make sure I reach the goals I've set for myself. I track my progress, content with the self-discipline applied to each goal along the way. As I get closer to achieving my goals, I see them more clearly. They become more distinct – so my concentration on them improves.

The older I get, I find it more necessary to refresh my memory of original plans and deadlines, and to kick in extra effort throughout the year. I refuse to become distracted from my goals, failing to see them fulfilled.

In much the same way, I've found that it is helpful to re-read parts of the bible on a regular basis. As I am reminded of the important stories that God has chosen to share with us, I see more and more detail that is meaningful when applied to my own life. Allowing my mind to be exposed to the truth on a regular basis and repeatedly studying God's words helps sharpen my focus on Him and imagine how God sees things and how He might be thinking about the circumstances I face.

It is inspiring to consider seeing things from His perspective, as much as my limited mind allows. And the more I soak in His truth, the less distracted I become – and the more I feel my love for Him at a deeper level than ever before. Falling in love does something to us – it brings intense focus. I would rather be passionate about "God things" than things in this world. When we put our relationship with Him first, our thinking is corrected and things around us seem to fall into place.

Second Corinthians 5:13-15 says, "If I acted crazy, I did it for God; if I acted overly serious, I did it for you. Christ's love has moved me to such extremes. His love has the first and last word in everything we do. Our firm decision is to work from this focused center: One man died for everyone. That puts everyone in the same boat. He included everyone in His death so that everyone could also be included in His life, a resurrection life, a far better life than people ever lived on their own."

If you've ever been "in love", you know the intensity of that focus. Let's refresh our thinking with God in that way from time to time. Revelation 2:4 talks about God's displeasure with a church that lost its "first love". He commands: "repent and do the things you did at first".

Over time, relationships deteriorate if constant effort is not applied to strengthen the relationship.

Take these steps to keep God your "first love":

Completely focus on Him, making the relationship with Him your first priority, spend time quietly listening for His direction, speak to Him about every detail of your life, and think about Him while studying the bible.

Take the relationship to a new level – tell Him you are sorry for things that have taken up your attention and actively work to remove those things from your life.

Re-focus on God's love for you and duplicate that love in dealing with others. You will find that your love for people will grow and you will have a sense of fulfillment and peace that only God can give.

John 16:33 says, "I have told you these things so that

in Me you may have perfect peace and confidence. In the world you have tribulation and trials and distress and frustration; but be of good cheer [take courage; be confident, certain, undaunted]! For I have overcome the world. [I have deprived it of power to harm you and have conquered it for you.]"

Blessed

"God bless you and keep you; God smile on you and gift you; God look you full in the face and make you prosper." (Numbers 6:24-26)

When we really understand how much God loves us, in spite of everything He knows about us, we cannot help but be comforted with an indescribable peace. Isaiah 49:16 says, "Behold, I have indelibly imprinted (tattooed a picture of) you on the palm of each of my hands." He knows and cares for us and He is continually aware of everything we face. That kind of compassion motivates me! It compels me to extend mercy to others, to forgive more freely and to love people I meet following to the example of Jesus.

Just think: God wants to be your friend and He is constantly thinking about you! He is excited to meet with you! Try to imagine how God desires to bless you and protect you. Doesn't that give you great courage in facing anything this world can throw at you?

The One who created us loves us even though He knows the worst characteristics within us and has seen us at our lowest moments.

He knows me better than I know myself and yet He is determined to provide for me abundantly beyond all that I could ask or imagine. Many of us have had a friend walk away from us when they see our weaknesses and experience our attitudes – but God knows all this and still desires to lavish His love upon us – that's what unconditional love is! It is so foreign to us as finite human beings, we find it hard to understand how to even receive that kind of love – much less how to give it away. We all know the story of the Prodigal Son – to refresh your memory, read Luke 15:11-32. At what point in that story do you think the father loved his son the most? And when did he love him the least? We can easily see the answers to those questions if we were that father, right? But the story is about our Heavenly Father, and His unconditional love for us never diminishes! As we often see ourselves as the prodigal son in that story, His love for us never changes. Our perception of His love for us stops us from receiving that love many times – but His love remains the same.

Now, how can we not humbly approach Him in worship and adoration understanding that kind of unconditional love He has for us? It's a covenant love – a promise that He will not break. My joy is made complete in Him - I can trust Him for all things and I can rest in the fact that His faithfulness to me will never end.

Love ya, but...

"We don't deserve praise! The LORD alone deserves all of the praise, because of His love and faithfulness.

Why should the nations ask, "Where is your God?" Our God is in the heavens, doing as He chooses. The idols of the nations are made of silver and gold. They have a mouth and eyes, but they can't speak or see. Their ears can't hear, and their noses can't smell. Their hands have no feeling, their legs don't move, and they can't make a sound. Everyone who made the idols and all who trust them are just as helpless as those useless gods." (Psalm 115:1-8)

I was convicted the other day when I remembered a saying that became popular from a commercial several years back: "I love ya man... but you're not getting my Bud." It was humorous in the commercial, but it is sad to consider how shallow our "love" for others really is sometimes. How quickly we offer words with no real meaning behind them. The words are easy to say, but often the devotion is absent. It is especially sad when we see the weak connection between telling God we love Him and then seeing what we offer Him. Sometimes we keep things back from Him because we think they provide us pleasure and happiness. Pleasure derived from what the world offers is fleeting. In reality, only God can provide true satisfaction and joy that lasts. Ephesians 4:1 admonishes each of us to "live a life worthy of the calling you have received."

As Americans we do not usually see physical structures like the idols portrayed in the bible or as seen in other cultures. But when we place our desires above God's commands, those things become idols to us. Whenever we refuse to give God everything, we have proven what we truly love – ourselves. Isaiah 64:4 says "Since before time began no one has ever imagined, No ear heard, no eye seen, a God like you who works for those who wait for Him." When we say we love Him, let's make sure we follow through with actions that would declare us guilty if we were convicted of being a Christian in a court of law. Consider how faithful God has been and seek to pursue holiness and the likeness of Jesus in every word and deed.

Psalm 37:3-4 says, "Trust (lean on, rely on, and be confident) in the Lord and do good; so shall you dwell in the land and feed surely on His faithfulness, and truly you shall be fed. Delight yourself also in the Lord, and He will give you the desires and secret petitions of your heart. Commit your way to the Lord [roll and repose each care of your load on Him]; trust also in Him and He will bring it to pass."

Relating Well

"A new command I give you: Love one another. As I have loved you, so you must love one another. By this all men will know that you are My disciples, if you love one another." (John 13:34-35)

God created us for relationships and He desires to meet people's needs through relationships – and He chose those in advance. Never look at the person, but separate the person from their behavior. If they act in a manner you consider inappropriate, what is that to you? That is between the person and God - show deep compassion for others the way Jesus did. We do not love only for the benefit of the other person, but when we love, we mature and become more like Christ, which is our goal! We have been sent to be His healing agents in this world. Do you bring comfort and reconciliation to those you see each day? People will identify us as followers of Jesus because of our fruit: love, joy, peace, patience, kindness, goodness, faithfulness, gentleness and self-control.

Sometimes we do not feel like loving those we face in difficult situations, but if God had to sacrifice His only begotten Son to extend His love to us (when He is perfect and we are sinners), we too should be more than willing to experience some discomfort in expressing God's love to others. Sacrifice means to consider the needs of others as more important than your own. We are not above God and superior to the law of loving others.

Our focus should be primarily on God and how He has treated us with so much grace and mercy. For me, it helps to remember the days when I wandered aimlessly, before God redeemed me, and then I try to extend the same kindness to others. God is pleased to see us love others in an attitude of thanks for all He has done for us – and He knows it is for our benefit when we love others – especially those who are difficult to love.

So by loving others, we worship God and draw closer to Him, who shows us how to love unconditionally. When we focus on God and not on ourselves, we are able to see past our selfish motives, to forgive freely and show pure love toward others generously.

Our prayers become pure when our focus is on God - then His love flows through us to others. Spending time in God's presence strengthens us with His joy, and that will overflow into the lives of those we touch on a daily basis. When we love, we obey God's command, and He can work miraculously through situations - bringing more people into His kingdom and bringing us closer to Him - in relationship and in likeness.

Good to Go

"For we are God's workmanship, created in Christ Jesus to do good works, which God prepared in advance for us to do." (Ephesians 2:10)

In the 10th chapter of Acts we see the story unfold of how God showed Peter that all men are created equal, pointing out the importance of not showing favoritism.

Peter had a vision revealing that all animals are created by God, and therefore considered clean (and, although not culturally accepted at the time, good to eat). This represents what is about to happen next when Peter visits with Cornelius, who is a Roman officer. Peter, being a Jew, had a meal and shared the gospel with the unbelieving friends and family of Cornelius - also not a culturally accepted activity at that time. Peter was being obedient to what the Lord had called him to do.

When we're obedient, God can move suddenly, as He did during Peter's sermon to Cornelius and his family when the Holy Spirit moved upon the hearts of those listening. Peter had moved out of his comfort zone and was focused on boldly speaking the truth about God and he was blessed as a result. We need to see others the way God sees them - to anticipate the need for the keys to the kingdom and always be ready to share with others the hope we have and the truth about Jesus.

We are equipped to reveal the truth about God when we consistently study His word and listen to the Holy

Spirit speaking to our hearts. We need to walk by faith, focusing on what is unseen (II Corinthians 4:18) because what we see with our eyes is only temporary and can be changed in a moment. Jonah 2:8 says, "Those who pay regard to false, useless, and worthless idols forsake their own [Source of] mercy and loving-kindness."

We need to focus on God by faith, obeying Him and experiencing the grace that He pours out on us. What we can see with our eyes, the world believes is true and real - but we know that it is only temporary. We need to set our gaze on Jesus - in this mentality, nothing can shake us or cause us to worry. Then others will be drawn to the kingdom of God when they witness the peace that we have in the midst of troubles. Romans 14:16-18 says, "Do not allow what you consider good to be spoken of as evil. For the kingdom of God is not a matter of eating and drinking, but of righteousness, peace and joy in the Holy Spirit, because anyone who serves Christ in this way is pleasing to God and approved by men."

God is equally available to all and He has called us to speak the truth in love to all people, regardless of where they are from, what they look like or how they might act. Always remember God's mercy toward you and reflect that mercy and compassion toward others - even if you are uncomfortable doing so - practice makes perfect! When we get in the habit of stepping out of our comfort zone in faith, it'll become easier to love others on a regular basis and we won't even consider our level of comfort at the time. Trust that God has a plan - be obedient and instead of focusing on your own inability, focus on God's ability - nothing is too difficult for Him! We've been grafted in as part of God's family, so we should be ready to look at others with compassion, so they will experience the love of God and be drawn to Him, learning how to relate to Him personally. Each person we see is an eternal soul moving toward God or toward an eternity without Him. Our focus should be on God's heart so we can share that compassion: "then make my joy complete by being like-minded, having the same love, being one in spirit and purpose. Do nothing out of selfish ambition or vain conceit, but in humility consider others better than yourselves. Each of you should look not only to your own interests, but also to the interests of others." (Phil 2:2-4)

Luke 6:35-36 says, "I tell you, love your enemies. Help and give without expecting a return. You'll never — I promise — regret it. Live out this God-created identity the way our Father lives toward us, generously and graciously, even when we're at our worst. Our Father is kind; you be kind.

In Acts 10:38, the word for "healing" originally used is "iaomia" which means "gradual healing", so even though God can change things suddenly, people generally change gradually over time. We need to remember that when we pray for others – we may not see change quickly in the people we are praying for, but God knows the end, and as we remain faithful in praying for and encouraging others, by faith we have to believe that God is doing a work in their hearts!

One of our greatest challenges in this life is to intentionally get dislodged from our comfort zone!

Jesus certainly exited His comfort zone for us by dying on the cross for our sins! Our perception has to change – instead of always thinking of ourselves, we should focus on other people and love them. God knows how to hit the "eject button" on our "La-Z-Boy" and get us moving in the right direction – that's why we can't get distracted from our time with Him, so we are always listening to His guidance and taking every opportunity that faces us each day to share the truth. We may only sow seeds into others' lives - or we may water the seed - or we may walk someone into a relationship with Jesus – but we need to be ready for any of those activities and the let the fruit of the spirit (Galatians 5:21-23) manifest and draw others to God.

Luke 14:12-14 says, "Then he turned to the host. 'The next time you put on a dinner, don't just invite your friends and family and rich neighbors, the kind of people who will return the favor. Invite some people who never get invited out, the misfits from the wrong side of the tracks. You'll be — and experience — a blessing. They won't be able to return the favor, but the favor will be returned — oh, how it will be returned! — at the resurrection of God's people.'"

Focus on intentionally stepping out of your comfort zone to actively touch others for God's kingdom and draw others to Jesus. It's not always fun at first, but in the end when you see God's hand working through it all, it is an awesome experience! God knows how to get our attention and when we're praying for wisdom to follow His will exactly as He has in mind, He will be faithful to direct us! God has accepted us and He is the lifter of our head! First Samuel 16:8 says, "The LORD does not look at the things man looks at. Man looks at the outward appearance, but the LORD looks at the heart."

Life Producing Waves

The king's heart is in the hand of the LORD; He directs it like a watercourse wherever He pleases. All a man's ways seem right to him, but the LORD weighs the heart. To do what is right and just is more acceptable to the LORD than sacrifice. (Prov. 21:1-3)

Have you ever stood in an ocean and just let the power of the waves push you around? In comparing life to waves, I recently learned a lesson… The waves go out to the depths of the ocean and gain their strength to return, crashing upon the shore. Imagine you are the wave, God is in the depths and the shoreline represents the people you influence in your lifetime. The depth of the ocean and the power of the wind determine the strength of waves washing up on shore.

Jesus describes to Nicodemus the influence of God's Spirit by comparing it with the wind. (John 3:8) "You know well enough how the wind blows this way and that. You hear it rustling through the trees, but you have no idea where it comes from or where it's headed next. That's the way it is with everyone 'born from above' by the wind of God, the Spirit of God."

I think much like the wind controls the size of waves in the ocean, God's Holy Spirit controls whose lives we affect and the power of our influence on others. The length of time we spend in God's presence - getting to know Him, talking to Him and listening for Him to speak to our hearts - will determine the way we affect others in our day to day relationships. And as we return to our activities after being with God, we have the opportunity to represent Jesus for those around us.

Make time to be with God every day – in His presence we find strength and courage, joy and compassion, purpose in reaching out in love to others. Then, as we "wash ashore" throughout our day, we minister to those around us while we walk in that strength that we receive from "being still" in God's presence. Regardless of how others respond to us or react to what we say and do, we need to be faithful to return to them and believe God is using us to impact their soul for eternity. Just as water is a powerful force and can change the course of a river, God wants to use us to change people's lives by His supernatural power flowing through us.

Our faithfulness to God sometimes wanes – but like the waves flowing back and forth, we need to return to Him and determine to do the right thing during this short time that we have here. Others are watching us and we will give an account some day for our influence on others. Rippling water can softly wash away the sand from our fingers, but also with persistence, it can wear down rough edges of the rocks on shore. Our lives can softly touch people's hearts when necessary, but God can also use us to effectively bring about change that would seem impossible in the natural. Just by being obedient, we can allow the Spirit of God to "blow us into His purposes" and grow the kingdom of God for His glory.

"A Christian worker is one who perpetually looks in the face of God and then goes forth to talk to people. The secret of the worker's life is that he keeps in tune with God all the time." (Oswald Chambers)

Roller Coaster Ride of Life

"I'll show up and take care of you as I promised and bring you back home. I know what I'm doing. I have it all planned out - plans to take care of you, not abandon you, plans to give you the future you hope for. When you call on Me, when you come and pray to Me, I'll listen. When you come looking for Me, you'll find Me. Yes, when you get serious about finding Me and want it more than anything else, I'll make sure you won't be disappointed." - God's Decree. "I'll turn things around for you. I'll bring you back from all the countries into which I drove you; bring you home to the place from which I sent you off into exile. You can count on it. God's Decree." (Jeremiah 29:11-13)

Many times we pray to our Heavenly Father for our really big problems, but only after all else fails. We need to take time each day to really focus on every hindrance, every concern and every problem we face, as well as those we see others facing, and give it all to God. Trust Him. He is a big God – NOTHING is too difficult for Him! When we learn to apply God's Word to every situation in life and maintain a readiness to share His truth to those along the way, we will see an amazing outcome. We often see relational problems as impossible situations since we have no control over other people, and we see the problem as hopeless... but God knit together the hearts of every person. He knows everything about us and He strategically positions each one where He wants. We cannot correctly judge the hearts of other people, but God can. So trust Him to turn the difficult situations around.

Just like when you get on a roller coaster at an amusement park and you brace yourself as the ride slowly takes off, knowing that you will soon be accelerating through loops and curves – that's kind of how I think it is to live in perfect communion with the Heavenly Father... You realize everything you do has been planned in advance for you – it's a wonderful adventure prepared by your Heavenly Father, who created you with a purpose and directs your steps and conversations according to His love for you. Brace yourself for an unbelievable ride! Anticipate great things to happen, but know there will be some surprises, too! He exceeds our expectations. Ask Him to open your eyes to see so you can grow through the process and watch Him take an ordinary situation and turn it into a beautiful expression of His love.

Romans 8:26-39 says it best: "Meanwhile, the moment we get tired in the waiting, God's Spirit is right alongside helping us along. If we don't know how or what to pray, it doesn't matter. He does our praying in and for us, making prayer out of our wordless sighs, our aching groans. He knows us far better than we know ourselves, knows our pregnant condition, and keeps us present before God. That's why we can be so sure that every detail in our lives of love for God is worked into something good."

"God knew what he was doing from the very

beginning. He decided from the outset to shape the lives of those who love Him along the same lines as the life of His Son. The Son stands first in the line of humanity He restored. We see the original and intended shape of our lives there in Him. After God made that decision of what His children should be like, He followed it up by calling people by name. After He called them by name, He set them on a solid basis with Himself. And then, after getting them established, He stayed with them to the end, gloriously completing what He had begun."

"So, what do you think? With God on our side like this, how can we lose? If God didn't hesitate to put everything on the line for us, embracing our condition and exposing Himself to the worst by sending his own Son, is there anything else He wouldn't gladly and freely do for us? And who would dare tangle with God by messing with one of God's chosen? Who would dare even to point a finger?"

"The One who died for us - who was raised to life for us! - is in the presence of God at this very moment sticking up for us. Do you think anyone is going to be able to drive a wedge between us and Christ's love for us? There is no way! Not trouble, not hard times, not hatred, not hunger, not homelessness, not bullying threats, not backstabbing, not even the worst sins listed in Scripture: They kill us in cold blood because they hate You. We're sitting ducks; they pick us off one by one. None of this fazes us because Jesus loves us."

"I'm absolutely convinced that nothing - nothing

living or dead, angelic or demonic, today or tomorrow, high or low, thinkable or unthinkable - absolutely nothing can get between us and God's love because of the way that Jesus our Master has embraced us."

Chapter Three – HOPE

The Canoe Ride of Life

"So here's what I want you to do, God helping you: Take your everyday, ordinary life - your sleeping, eating, going-to-work, and walking-around life - and place it before God as an offering. Embracing what God does for you is the best thing you can do for Him. Don't become so well-adjusted to your culture that you fit into it without even thinking. Instead, fix your attention on God. You'll be changed from the inside out. Readily recognize what He wants from you, and quickly respond to it. Unlike the culture around you, always dragging you down to its level of immaturity, God brings the best out of you, develops well-formed maturity in you." (Romans 12:1-2)

I love watching the river's current as it runs along and splashes on the banks, sometimes drawing twigs and leaves into the river along the way. The turbulence of the splashing waves drives everything down current and eventually to the bottom of the river. If you happen to be in a canoe, it may cause you to drift into trees and branches along the way. That is how our enemy works – the one whose goal is to kill, steal and destroy – loves to bring tough situations into our lives at every turn and take us to the bottom.

We can take a less from the Salmon: they run against the flow, feeling their way in opposition to the water's forceful current and the patterns of rippling water.

They "smell" their way upstream to complete their life cycle and prepare the way for their young to survive.

Their goal is set and nothing deters them from reaching it, although they face many difficulties along the way. They are focused as they fulfill their "vision" – and once they reach their goal their life is complete.

We would do well if we followed the example of their behavior in our own life.

Our Creator longs for us to have a relationship with Him. In our pursuit of God - we need to die to ourselves and go against the flow of our culture.

We are faced with many distractions that divert our attention away from our goals, especially when it comes to the goal of spiritual maturity. Stay focused on your vision. You were created with a purpose and gifted to complete that task. Never give up, never doubt, never lose hope. A wise man once said, "God will pull you through anything, if you can stand the pull." He'll guide the way.

If you have ever chased after a toddler about to step into a busy street, you know what it is to be focused.

In those moments, you do not hear anything or see anything except your goal: to remove the child from that dangerous situation. That's how we need to pursue God.

Remove every distraction in life, moving toward the goal: to know God's heart, to study the truth in His word, to hear His voice, to follow the path He has for us, to grow in maturity into the likeness of Jesus Christ, to approach a life of holiness.

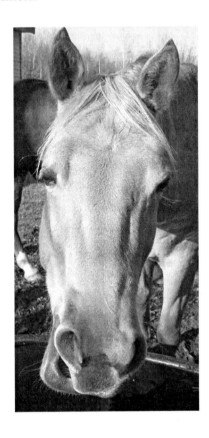

Seek God's Vision

"Remember the former things, those of long ago; I am God, and there is no other; I am God and there is none like Me. I make known the end from the beginning, from ancient times, what is still to come. I say: My purpose will stand, and I will do all that I please. From the east I summon a bird of prey; from a far-off land, a man to fulfill My purpose. What I have said, that will I bring about; what I have planned, that will I do." (Isaiah 46:9-11)

When God created you, He had a vision. There was a purpose in the way He designed you: every aspect of your being was a part of His plan and He saw each of your days before you ever took your first step (Psalm 139:13-16). He knows the end from the beginning and He considered everything you would face in life as He established you. Your unique personality, the color of your skin and the culture you were placed in were all in the mind of our Creator as He carefully and intentionally designed you to be the person you are. Press in closer to Him to determine the plan He has for you and you will not be disappointed when you see His plan come to fruition. He's not finished with you yet.

His ways include using other people, through relationships, to shape you into the person He created you to be. We derive our most fundamental sense of identity by relating to God and others. We must appreciate His original plan to make us in His image as we relate to one another. According to Ephesians 3:14-21, we have the fullness of God when we are rightly relating to one another within His family - that is, all who believe in Him. That is the only way to truly understand His love: how wide it is – covering the breadth of our own experience and reaching out to the whole world; how long it is – continuing throughout the length of our lives; how high it is – rising to the heights of our greatest moments, life's most exciting events; how deep it is – reaching to the depths of our discouragement, loneliness, loss, moments of despair and even to the very end at our death, His love remains. As we depend on our friends within our community, we begin to understand the majesty and love of God. He takes those who are all alone and He places them in families. I have to relate to others in order to become all that He has planned – perfect holiness demands my relating well with people – focusing on others and totally selfless.

True Reflections

"And we, who with unveiled faces all reflect the Lord's glory, are being transformed into His likeness with ever-increasing glory, which comes from the Lord, who is the Spirit." (II Corinthians 3:18)

There is a commercial that refers to the source of high definition light by saying "it's the mirrors". Some people prefer not to look into mirrors because it is an honest reflection of who they are. We are taught to look into the bible and apply that truth to our lives: (James 1:22-24) Do not merely listen to the word, and so deceive yourselves. Do what it says. Anyone who listens to the word but does not do what it says is like a man who looks at his face in a mirror and, after looking at himself, goes away and immediately forgets what he looks like.

God wants us to resemble Him – He created us in His image. Proverbs 27:19 says "As water reflects a face, so a man's heart reflects the man." When we follow His plan and become more like Him, others will be drawn by Him and to Him, as we reflect who God truly is. God's light reflected in mirrors will clearly direct your path.

Study His word – look into it as you would a mirror to honestly see who He is so you can become an honest reflection of Him. Remember He is a jealous God, so stay true to Him. The battle is the Lord's. Give your concerns to Him and trust Him to take over and watch Him work – He will deliver you! He longs to tell you "Everything is going to be OK." It's already been taken care of – we are the victors! Trust in Him and He will lead you through to victory!

Mentoring a Disciple

"Do your best to present yourself to God as one approved, a workman who does not need to be ashamed and who correctly handles the word of truth." (II Timothy 2:15)

To reach out to others and fulfill the purposes for which we're called requires us to rely completely on God's strength being made perfect in our weaknesses (by His grace and because of His great love for us). Speaking from experience, I'll share what I learned as I look back on the influence of those who mentored me through various parts of my life.

God frequently chooses to reveal Himself through relationships, so we need to seriously consider how our words and actions toward others will affect them. Many times our words are more powerful than we think. Proverbs says life and death are in the power of the tongue, so we need to speak carefully, considering the effects of our words on others.

Showing mercy and compassion to others will quickly drain us as we listen to the problems of people around us if we don't first soak in quiet time together with God. Pointing others toward a closer relationship with Jesus Christ often requires supernatural strength.

We need to listen and sincerely care about those who look to us for explaining the truth to them – which requires our time and emotion while we wait to hear God's Spirit direct us to gently speak the truth in love.

As you meet with others and discuss life's joys and struggles, you must exemplify the love of Christ – and others will be drawn to Jesus as a result. Pray first, then live out the life Jesus taught by example in the New Testament. As others witness our prayers being answered, God will become more real to them, and their faith will grow. We have been adopted into God's family and He calls us His friend, so we have great faith and confidence that He will answer our prayers – this is remarkable to others when they see this relationship lived out, and they will want to know God like you do when they realize the peace and joy that comes from living in such close communion with Him.

Your transparency helps others see they can be authentic before God and learn that they don't have to be perfect - or even pretend to be perfect! God sees us as we really are - and when we're sincerely committed to following Him, it is His pleasure to help us become more like Him.

Luke 12:31-32 says, "Only aim at and strive for and seek His kingdom, and all these things shall be supplied to you also. Do not be seized with alarm and struck with fear, little flock, for it is your Father's good pleasure to give you the kingdom!"

Pray together with others whenever the opportunity arises, and they will see our Heavenly Father as a personable God they can talk to when people aren't available - and if they listen carefully and concentrate on Him enough, they will learn to "hear" Him speaking to their heart.

As people grow and mature in their relationship with the Lord, they will prefer talking to God many times, instead of other people, for life's answers. God wants us to share our ideas, concerns, needs and joys with Him, without being afraid of Him. He will reveal His love, mercy and compassion as we confess our mistakes and seek His forgiveness in prayer.

Second Timothy 2:22 says, "Flee the evil desires of youth, and pursue righteousness, faith, love and peace, along with those who call on the Lord out of a pure heart."

We can never give up on our friends and family regardless of how impossible the situation may appear to us. Focus on God's ability – He cannot fail – instead of the inabilities people have. We can be confident that God, Our Creator and Savior, understands us!

Perfect love casts away fear and God's love for us is perfect – it is unconditional. We need to portray that unconditional love to others so they will be comfortable freely talking to God about everything, and move toward growing up in Him. You will never know how much your advice and time spent with others affects them in the long run.

It may take many years, but God's Word does not return void – it accomplishes what He sets it forth to achieve. When we speak the truth into another person's life, the seed is planted and over time, it will sprout forth new life.

II Timothy 3:14-17 says, "But as for you, continue in

what you have learned and have become convinced of, because you know those from whom you learned it, and how from infancy you have known the holy Scriptures, which are able to make you wise for salvation through faith in Christ Jesus. All Scripture is God-breathed and is useful for teaching, rebuking, correcting and training in righteousness, so that the man of God may be thoroughly equipped for every good work."

Focus

"If you have raced with men on foot and they have worn you out, how can you compete with horses? If you stumble in safe country, how will you manage in the thickets by the Jordan?" (Jeremiah 12:5)

Whatever we choose to focus on is what becomes real and large in our minds. We choose what we think about – and our thoughts turn into actions eventually. That is why the bible says: "Summing it all up, friends, I'd say you'll do best by filling your minds and meditating on things true, noble, reputable, authentic, compelling, gracious - the best, not the worst; the beautiful, not the ugly; things to praise, not things to curse . Put into practice what you learned from me, what you heard and saw and realized. Do that, and God, who makes everything work together, will work you into his most excellent harmonies." (Philippians 4:8)

When we focus on the qualities and abilities of God, we cannot worry; we will not stumble. Nothing is beyond His ability to heal, fix, provide for – He is never surprised by the events of the day. And He sees things differently than we see them – because there is a spiritual realm that we cannot see with our eyes. We need to stand in faith believing that God is in control of everything and obey Him even when it doesn't seem to make sense. We know that without faith it's impossible to please God (Hebrews 11:6) and Romans 14:23 says that whatever is not of faith, is sin.

Ephesians 6:11-13 says "And that about wraps it up.

God is strong, and he wants you strong. So take everything the Master has set out for you, well-made weapons of the best materials. And put them to use so you will be able to stand up to everything the Devil throws your way. This is no afternoon athletic contest that we'll walk away from and forget about in a couple of hours. This is for keeps, a life-or-death fight to the finish against the Devil and all his angels. Be prepared. You're up against far more than you can handle on your own. Take all the help you can get, every weapon God has issued, so that when it's all over but the shouting you'll still be on your feet. Truth, righteousness, peace, faith, and salvation are more than words. Learn how to apply them. You'll need them throughout your life. God's Word is an indispensable weapon. In the same way, prayer is essential in this ongoing warfare. Pray hard and long. Pray for your brothers and sisters. Keep your eyes open. Keep each other's spirits up so that no one falls behind or drops out."

Remember that God is working out His plan for things greater than we can even imagine – and that the victory is already ours when we obey Him! We need to keep our eyes off the things we see that are temporary and focus on God's kingdom. Focus on the eternal by faith and see God walking alongside you to help you along the way! I Jn 4:4 ~ "My dear children, you come from God and belong to God. You have already won a big victory over those false teachers, for the Spirit in you is far stronger than anything in the world."

Our Source of Hope

"My soul magnifies the Lord, And my spirit has rejoiced in God my Savior… For He who is mighty has done great things for me, And holy is His name. And His mercy is on those who fear Him From generation to generation. He has shown strength with His arm; He has scattered the proud in the imagination of their hearts. He has put down the mighty from their thrones, and exalted the lowly. He has filled the hungry with good things, and the rich He has sent away empty." (Luke 1:46-53)

There is a hymn we commonly sing at Christmas time that tells the story of the birth of Jesus: *O little town of Bethlehem, how still we see thee lie! Above thy deep and dreamless sleep the silent stars go by. Yet in thy dark streets shineth the everlasting Light; The hopes and fears of all the years are met in thee tonight. For Christ is born of Mary, and gathered all above, While mortals sleep, the angels keep their watch of wondering love. O morning stars together, proclaim the holy birth, And praises sing to God the King, and peace to men on earth! How silently, how silently, the wondrous Gift is giv'n; So God imparts to human hearts the blessings of His Heav'n. No ear may hear His coming, but in this world of sin, Where meek souls will receive Him still, the dear Christ enters in.*

The lyrics to the hymn ring true: *how silently*. God did not bring Himself to earth with a loud celebration, clanging of cymbals or riding a white horse. He did not announce His coming with flashing lights or trumpets.

God does not change - this is still how God comes to us – silently, in a still, small voice, quietly - as we reflect on Him. God doesn't come to us in bolts of lightening and a thundering voice from heaven. God can do that, but that's not His normal way of communicating. He comes to us when we're quiet and He speaks to our hearts. A verse of Scripture comes to our mind or we find ourselves reading a passage of God's Word, or a friend tells us about seeing the love of God expressed and silently, almost undetected, God brings His Son to us.

"O holy Child of Bethlehem, descend to us, we pray; Cast out our sin, and enter in, be born in us today. We hear the Christmas angels the great glad tidings tell; O come to us, abide with us, our Lord Emmanuel! O little town of Bethlehem, how still we see thee lie! Above thy deep and dreamless sleep the silent stars go by. Yet in thy dark streets shineth the everlasting Light; The hopes and fears of all the years are met in thee tonight."

My favorite part of this hymn is the last line: "The hopes and fears of all the years are met in Thee tonight." What a huge statement! How comforting when you think about it! We all struggle with fears at some point throughout our lives. Some may fear death. Others may fear a report from the doctor. Many may fear financial difficulties in life. You may be afraid of your boss at work or a teacher at school or a bully at school. Fears are real and they're constant and they're right here. The more we focus on them, the bigger they get. Sometimes they feel overwhelming, like they're suffocating us or almost like we can touch them. But the Christmas carol, "O Little Town of Bethlehem" tells us how to conquer those fears. Because the fears of all the years and the hopes of all the years are met in a single Person, Jesus. Give Him your fears. "Cast your care on Him, because He cares for you", and find your hope in Him. In Him you will find eternal life, and that makes life worth living now. When He gives you His favor, you will know that this is just a trial run, a preparation for eternity – and our current problems are nothing when you look at them from His perspective and see all that He has in store for your future!

"His divine power has given us everything we need for life and godliness through our knowledge of him who called us by his own glory and goodness." (II Peter 1:3)

The Great Adventure

"Don't bargain with God. Be direct. Ask for what you need. This is not a cat-and-mouse, hide-and-seek game we're in. If your little boy asks for a serving of fish, do you scare him with a live snake on his plate? If your little girl asks for an egg, do you trick her with a spider? As bad as you are, you wouldn't think of such a thing – you're at least decent to your own children. And don't you think the Father who conceived you in love will give the Holy Spirit when you ask Him?" (Luke 11:10-13)

We, who have recognized Jesus as our Savior and asked Him to be Lord of our life, have the significant privilege of asking for His help in this life. The bible was given for our benefit today! It is not a list of rules to follow in life to make us miserable, but it is a "benefits manual" for those who love the Lord with all their heart (Deuteronomy 6:5-6) and obey Him.

If you want to know how to get ahead in life, just pray for wisdom on a regular basis. The Holy Spirit is our counselor and teaches us all things – if we will ask. Study the Lord's prayer and what He teaches about prayer in Matthew 6, and see that God wants a deeper relationship with you. Continually strive to know Him more – and challenge yourself to believe He loves you more than you ever thought before – because He does! And just when you think you can grasp how great His love for you is, think again – He loves you more than you can imagine.

He gives without limit – so continue to expand your understanding of His completely unconditional love for you. We cannot fathom how much He loves us. In John 17, Jesus prays for His disciples (that's us) and gives us a great example of how a relationship with God helps us to pray for others and bless people we don't even know!

John 17:20 says, "My prayer is not for them alone. I pray also for those who will believe in Me through their message, that all of them may be one, Father, just as You are in Me and I am in You. May they also be in Us so that the world may believe that You have sent Me."

Pray to your Heavenly Father knowing He loves you and wants to draw closer to you and you will be amazed at how real God becomes to you, how much He loves you and how closely He will relate to you. We have no idea how much power is available when we tap into prayer, especially prayer in unity with others and with God's will. Max Lucado said, "Your prayers move God to change the world. You may not understand the mystery of prayer. You don't need to. But this much is clear: Actions in heaven begin when someone prays on earth. What an amazing thought!" I love to think about that!

The Favor of God

"For as a prince hast thou power with God and with men, and hast prevailed." (Genesis 32:28)

Those who resolve to put their trust in God obtain favor with God. As we talk to Him about the details of our life and seek His guidance and help, we become more than conquerors. He loves to see us put our faith in Him for every matter that concerns us. With God all things are possible... Apart from Him we can do nothing (see Hebrews 11:6, Mark 10:27, John 15). So, it is through prayer we obtain all the inexhaustible resources that are ours in Christ.

Get to know Him more each day and find His purpose for your life. He will give you joy and peace – commodities in short supply and mostly unfamiliar to those who do not yet know Him. Your effectiveness in life clearly correlates with your awareness of God's leading. Do you take time to listen and recognize His still, small voice? No one can lead you to excellence as well as your Creator!

Ephesians 3:16-20 says, "I pray that out of His glorious riches He may strengthen you with power through His Spirit in your inner being, so that Christ may dwell in your hearts through faith. And I pray that you, being rooted and established in love, may have power, together with all the saints, to grasp how wide and long and high and deep is the love of Christ, and to know this love that surpasses knowledge – that you may be filled to the measure of all the fullness of God. Now to Him who is able to do immeasurably more than all we ask or imagine, according to His power that is at work within us, to Him be glory in the church and in Christ Jesus throughout all generations, forever and ever! Amen."

What You Represent

"O Lord, You have searched me and known me. You comprehend my path and my lying down, And are acquainted with all my ways. Where can I go from You Spirit? Or where can I flee from Your presence? For You formed my inward parts; You covered me in my mother's womb. I will praise You, for I am fearfully and wonderfully made; Marvelous are Your works and that my soul knows very well. Your eyes saw my substance, being yet unformed, and in Your book they all were written, the days fashioned for me, when as yet there were none of them. How precious also are Your thoughts to me, O God! How great is the sum of them! If I should count them, they would be more in number than the sand; When I awake, I am still with You." (Psalm 139:1, 3, 7, 13-14, 16-18)

When I was young, I memorized a poem entitled "If Jesus Came to Your House". I am often reminded of that poem when I see things in my life I wouldn't want Jesus to witness – but He does. We are so limited in our understanding – He sees into our very soul. He knows everything about us – He knows us better than we know ourselves. We are prone to deceive ourselves in comparing our lives with others. We should only compare our life with that of Jesus and strive to be more like Him. One day we will see Him face to face. We should get rid of those things now that we wouldn't want Him to see – because

He already sees them. We will automatically be closer to Him the moment we put aside the things we think we want here on earth.

He longs to be intimately united with us and give us eternal blessings. We don't need to keep our distance thinking, "I cannot understand Him". He is an infinite God – and He can do immeasurably beyond anything we could ask or imagine – but He created us for relationship with Himself. God created the universe, then He created us - in His image. He enjoyed His creation and He wants us to enjoy it. Let Him be your closest confidant. Live your life to bring honor and glory to Him. Don't just live in mediocrity… Live abundantly! Break through the standard way of life and reach for a higher way of life. You represent the Creator of the Universe! You were created in the image of God, who is the King of Kings!

Where to Look

"I lift up my eyes to the hills – where does my help come from? My help comes from the Lord, the Maker of heaven and earth. He will not let your foot slip – He who watches over you will not slumber; indeed, He who watches over Israel will neither slumber nor sleep. The Lord watches over you – the Lord is your shade at your right hand; the sun will not harm you by day, nor the moon by night. The Lord will keep you from all harm – He will watch over your life; the Lord will watch over your coming and going both now and forevermore." (Psalm 121)

We should never think that God - our Creator, the Author and Perfecter of our faith, Lover of our soul, Rock of our salvation, our Provider – has forgotten us or overlooked us, or any detail of our life, for any period of time. When we take refuge in His mercy, truth and power, we can be confident that He will fulfill His promises to us. He has loved us with an everlasting love and promised He would never leave us nor forsake us. People will let us down occasionally – and we will be offended by others in our life every now and then, but look up! Nothing has changed in our relationship with our loving Heavenly Father – and He is the only One from whom we need approval. We have to continue to love our brothers and sisters – and we can when we focus on God's love for us.

I John 4:9 says we love because He first loved us. We are compelled to "overflow" with love because of our hope in Him. "We know that we have passed from death to life because we love our brothers. Anyone who does not love remains in death." (I John 3:14)

We have an everlasting covenant with God - which was His idea! - to guarantee His promises to us. The definition of covenant is "a binding and solemn agreement to do or keep from doing a specified thing, a formal, sealed contract; theologically, the promise made by God to humanity and the relationship it established, as described in the Bible. 2 a: a written agreement or promise usually under seal between two or more parties especially for the performance of some action, a pledge."

By virtue of His nature, God cannot lie – His actions are in accordance with His Word – He is truth. We need to fully rely on Him for everything – "what can man do to me?" We cannot look at the financial state of our nation and worry if we believe that God is our Provider. Our actions must reflect our belief – if we believe the bible is truth then we have peace knowing "God takes care of His own".

Psalms 91 says God "will give His angels special charge over you to accompany and defend and preserve you in all your ways [of obedience and service]."

Read Psalm 118:1, 5-8, 14-15: Give thanks to the Lord, for He is good; His love endures forever. In my anguish I cried to the Lord, and He answered by setting me free. The Lord is with me; I will not be afraid. What can man do to me? The Lord is with me; He is my helper. I will look in triumph on my enemies. It is better to take refuge in the Lord than to trust in man. The Lord is my strength and my song; He has become my salvation. Shouts of joy and victory resound in the tents of the righteous: The Lord's right hand has done mighty things!

Finding Meaning in Tradition

"Glory to God in the highest [heaven], and on earth peace among men with whom He is well pleased [men of goodwill, of His favor]." (Luke 2:14)

In the past, many times I would skim over the Christmas season without really "diving in" wholeheartedly. It was an event that would pass – an item on my list to cross off, in time. I didn't like what Christmas had become in this culture and I didn't want to be a part of it.

I didn't like to associate Christmas with merely monetary gifts, worrying if the recipient will be pleased with what I had chosen for them.

Something was missing – I just wanted to get past it and on into the new year.

We can't seem to prioritize the important things in life, so we try to make up for it with "stuff". Christmas is one time in the year that I would love to spend somewhere else on the globe. I love my family, but I'd like to see how people "celebrate" who do not have the means to participate in the commercialized frenzy we see in North America.

But I've softened more recently, and I've learned that the "Christmas songs" that I hated to hear as early as Halloween, are necessary to prepare my heart for the real meaning in Christmas. It takes time to reflect on what God originally intended, and the old hymns and

Christmas songs that portray the story of Jesus' birth help me to see the beauty throughout the season.

I enjoy watching young children at Christmas time – they just naturally express the joy, surprise and wonder of the season. Their pure little hearts are not tainted with selfishness; they do not envy or boast in their gifts. They aren't jealous of others' gifts or whine that they didn't get what they expected. They appreciate what's important and enjoy being surrounded by loving friends and family. They don't have mixed feelings about family members yet; to them, "family" is made up of the people who love them the most, with whom they are comfortable to freely express themselves. They do not play mind games with others, but show sincere love and joy – they color their scenes and make their little craft projects: Jesus in a manger for the nativity scene is central to the meaning of Christmas for them. They make angels in the snow and put the star on top of the Christmas tree – all significant items in the real Christmas story!

How do we, then, get so far off track by the time we become adults? We allow the distractions to multiply until Christmas means flying around the countryside, meeting with different parts of the family to consume different parts of a bird until we're so full of food and fellowship that we race home at the end of the day, exhausted by all the events – and usually glad that it's over. The "fun" part was our shopping sprees that we no longer want to remember – and we pray the post office will lose the bills arriving in our mailboxes for just a few months.

Reflecting on the lyrics of hymns that depict the real Christmas spirit, we are confronted with simplicity, peace, meaning, hope and love! Just try to imagine Christmas like this:

"Hark! The herald angels sing, "Glory to the newborn King; Peace on earth, and mercy mild, God and sinners reconciled!" Christ, by highest Heav'n adored; Christ the everlasting Lord; Late in time, behold Him come, Offspring of a virgin's womb. Veiled in flesh the Godhead see; Hail th'incarnate Deity, Pleased as man with men to dwell, Jesus our Emmanuel. Hail the heav'n born Prince of Peace! Hail the Sun of Righteousness! Light and life to all He brings, Ris'n with healing in His wings. Mild He lays His glory by, Born that man no more may die. Born to raise the sons of earth, Born to give them second birth.

The angels say to us, "Listen everyone! God (who is holy) is prepared to accept us (who are corrupt) to Himself through the birth of this Person, Jesus."

God gave us His best as a sacrifice. Jesus didn't come to Earth to put Bethlehem on the map. He didn't come to Earth to make you feel good, spend too much money or overindulge on ham and fruitcake at Christmas time.

Jesus came to Earth to reconcile opposing parties, God and you. He offers peace, through Jesus, to us who receive the gift of the Savior. He grants us His favor!

Col 2:9 ~ For in Christ all the fullness of the Deity lives in bodily form, and you have been given fullness in Christ, who is the head over every power and authority.

God's Faithfulness

"Do you see what this means — all these pioneers who blazed the way, all these veterans cheering us on? It means we'd better get on with it. Strip down, start running — and never quit! No extra spiritual fat, no parasitic sins. Keep your eyes on Jesus, who both began and finished this race we're in. Study how He did it. Because He never lost sight of where He was headed — that exhilarating finish in and with God — He could put up with anything along the way: Cross, shame, whatever. And now He's there, in the place of honor, right alongside God. When you find yourselves flagging in your faith, go over that story again, item by item, that long litany of hostility He plowed through. That will shoot adrenaline into your souls!" (Heb 12:1-3)

I've noticed that when I consistently go "above and beyond" the call of duty, then my reasonable acts of service and responsibilities that are expected of me seem easy! In the same way, when I have consistently lagged behind and slacked off in life, it gets harder and harder to reach the "status quo" and meet the requirements that are necessary for life. Jesus taught us to go the second mile: Matt 5:39-41 says, "But I tell you, Do not resist an evil person. If someone strikes you on the right cheek, turn to him the other also. And if someone wants to sue you and take your tunic, let him have your cloak as well. If someone forces you to go one mile, go with him two miles." It's not difficult to go beyond the expected once you build the habit – and the reward will be well worth it!

Jesus instructed us to act with mercy and compassion toward others. Going the second mile means not just praying for your friends and family, but lifting up people in positions of leadership as well as potential "enemies" in your life. Continually pray for the president, your boss, the CEO of your corporation, the annoying co-worker or neighbor, the chef who cooks your meal when you go out to dinner, the pilot on the plane when you travel, etc. Since we are to be in constant communication with our Heavenly Father, there is no limit to those we can be praying for, and know that God hears those prayers. Oswald Chambers said "Intercessory prayer for one who is sinning prevails. God says so! The will of the man prayed for does not come into question at all. He is connected with God by prayer, and prayer on the basis of Redemption sets the connection working and God gives life." That is so powerful!

We remember where we were when God lifted us out of the pit on our path to destruction –trust Him to be "mighty to save" those who seem lost beyond hope. S. T. Coleridge said, "The Jews would not willingly tread upon the smallest piece of paper in their way, but took it up; for possibly, they say, the name of God may be on it. Though there was a little superstition in this, yet truly there is nothing but good religion in it, if we apply it to men. Trample not on any; there may be some work of grace there, that thou knowest not of. The name of God may be written upon that soul thou treadest on; it may be a soul that Christ thought so much of, as to give His precious blood for it; therefore despise it not." Nothing is too difficult for God – do you really believe that? And do your prayers reflect your complete trust in Him? Romans 14:23 says "that which is not of faith is sin [wrong]".

Jesus died for us when we were hopelessly lost – now let us act accordingly and treat others with that same grace and mercy – lift them up in prayer and entrust their eternal souls to God by the power of His precious Holy Spirit. You will see wonders as you increase your level of trust in God: "In prayer the Church has received power to rule the world. The Church is always the little flock. But if it would stay together on its knees, it would dominate world politics – from the prayer room" (O. Hallesby). We don't need to understand how prayer works, but trust that God hears and acts when you take time to lift your requests up to Him. People need to see the power that is available in true Christianity through a dynamic and authentic relationship with our Heavenly Father, the Creator of heaven and earth, the Author and Perfecter of our faith (Heb 12:2).

When we pray, we need to trust in the character of God – we know His nature when we look at the bible – study the different names of God and find their true meaning. God is just and loving, slow to anger, and compassionate. He hears us when we call to Him and He understands. He is faithful to answer us – and even though His timing may not agree with ours, His purposes prevail. In His wisdom and patience, He allows for the salvation of everyone. He knows the hearts of the people He created. He designed us and knows the motives within us – we need to trust Him more than ourselves. He will provide every time. God has made a name for Himself – and we need to learn that we can depend on Him! His love for us is beyond our comprehension, so put your hope in Him today for everything.

Nehemiah 9 says, "You sent miraculous signs and wonders against Pharaoh, against all his officials and all the people of his land, for You knew how arrogantly the Egyptians treated them. You made a name for Yourself, which remains to this day. In their hunger, You gave them bread from heaven and in their thirst, You brought them water from the rock; You told them to go in and take possession of the land You had sworn with uplifted hand to give them. They refused to listen and failed to remember the miracles You performed among them. They became stiff-necked and in their rebellion appointed a leader in order to return to their slavery.

But You are a forgiving God, gracious and compassionate; slow to anger and abounding in love. Therefore You did not desert them. Forty years You sustained them in the wilderness, so that they lacked nothing; their clothes did not wear out and their feet did not swell. But they were disobedient and rebelled against You; they put Your law behind their backs.

They killed Your prophets, who had admonished them in order to turn them back to You; they committed awful blasphemies. So You handed them over to their enemies, who oppressed them. But when they were oppressed they cried out to You. From heaven You heard them, and in Your great compassion You gave them deliverers, who rescued them from the hand of their enemies. But as soon as they were at rest, they again did what was evil in Your sight. Then You abandoned them to the hand of their enemies so that they ruled over them.

And when they cried out to You again, You heard from heaven, and in Your compassion You delivered them time after time. Now therefore, O our God, the great, mighty and awesome God, who keeps His covenant of love, do not let all this hardship seem trifling in your eyes — the hardship that has come upon us, upon our kings and leaders, upon our priests and prophets, upon our fathers and all Your people, from the days of the kings of Assyria until today. In all that has happened to us, You have been just; You have acted faithfully, while we did wrong.

Mysteries

"In him we have redemption through His blood, the forgiveness of sins, in accordance with the riches of God's grace that He lavished on us with all wisdom and understanding. And He made known to us the mystery of His will according to His good pleasure, which He purposed in Christ, to be put into effect when the times will have reached their fulfillment - to bring all things in heaven and on earth together under one head, even Christ." (Ephesians 1:7-10)

Sometimes our life is filled with activities, thoughts and events that we don't understand. I like the song out by Sanctus Real, "Whatever You're Doing". The lyrics are so applicable to life sometimes: "There's a wave that's crashing over me; all I can do is surrender.

Whatever You're doing inside of me, it feels like chaos, but somehow there's peace. It's hard to surrender to what I can't see, but I'm giving in to something Heavenly."

When we don't see the big picture, it's hard to imagine where life is taking us, but we need to continue to trust that it isn't just "fate"... God, who loves us and created us and knows everything about us, guides our footsteps. He does everything with excellence, so we don't have to worry that our life will become a mess when we're committed to obediently following Him.

We have to trust Him knowing He is at work behind

the scenes. The times we spend wondering where He is taking us is for our benefit as well. When we feel like we're in the dark, we draw closer to God and He speaks to us when we are quieted by life's questions.

"I beg you to have patience with everything unresolved in your heart and try to love the questions themselves... Don't search for the answers, which could not be given to you now... the point is, to live everything. Live the questions now." - Rainer Maria Rilke

We work with Jesus to bring Him glory in everything, but He is the one making sure it all works out perfectly.

He is up to something bigger than us, and only God can pull it off for His purposes.

We need to continually re-evaluate our identity in Him, who He created us to be, and repeatedly surrender to His will. Seek to know His heart, ask for wisdom and obey His teaching. Then sit back and watch what He does!

Daniel 2:47-48 says, "The king said to Daniel, 'Surely your God is the God of gods and the Lord of kings and a revealer of mysteries, for you were able to reveal this mystery.' Then the king placed Daniel in a high position and lavished many gifts on him. He made him ruler over the entire province of Babylon and placed him in charge of all its wise men."

He reveals to us His truth as we set time aside to really press in to know Him and to talk to Him and ask Him for understanding: Colossians 2:2-3 says, "My purpose is that they may be encouraged in heart and united in love, so that they may have the full riches of complete understanding, in order that they may know the mystery of God, namely, Christ, in whom are hidden all the treasures of wisdom and knowledge."

Chapter Four – PEACE

God's Open Door Policy

"By day the Lord directs His love, at night His song is with me – a prayer to the God of my life." (Psalm 42:8)

When things in life do not make sense, I am reminded of Psalm 3:5-6: "Trust God from the bottom of your heart; don't try to figure out everything on your own. Listen for God's voice in everything you do, everywhere you go; He's the one who will keep you on track". It's comforting to know sometimes that when I don't know what to do, I can rest in knowing God does know what to do. It's amazing to realize that He cares enough about us to carry us along when we cannot muster enough strength to go on ourselves. His understanding of our predicament is greater than we realize.

I remember my grandma asking me when I was seven years old if I knew how old my dad was. My young mind was normally good with numbers, but I didn't realize their values, as indicated by my answer "He's either 37 or 73." I was quite proud of the fact that I knew his approximate age and confused at the laughter that followed my response. The difference between his age and mine seemed so monumental to me at the time that 37 and 73 were equally representative of the age of someone much older than me. When we consider the difference between the understanding of a 7-year-old and an adult, how much greater is the difference between our wisdom and God's! We cannot even come close to imagining the depth of understanding of our Heavenly Father or the great chasm between our knowledge and His. I am grateful for what I do know about Him - and what I do know continually leads me to strive to know more about Him. It seems like the more I learn, the more I realize I do not know anything.

The bible teaches us how to acquire knowledge, wisdom and understanding: (Proverbs. 2:6) "For the Lord gives wisdom, and from His mouth come knowledge and understanding." (Proverbs 4:10-12) "Listen, my son, accept what I say, and the years of your life will be many. I guide you in the way of wisdom and lead you along straight paths. When you walk, your steps will not be hampered; when you run, you will not stumble." (Proverbs 9:10-11) "The reverent and worshipful fear of the Lord is the beginning (the chief and choice part) of Wisdom, and the knowledge of the Holy One is insight and understanding. For by me [Wisdom from God] your days shall be multiplied, and the years of your life shall be increased."

God is our source for wisdom and He never tires of helping us when we seek more wisdom. He is always available when we call out to Him. He never runs out of ideas – that's why we call Him "our Creator" – He is continually creating new things. The more time we spend with Him, the more creative we become, too! His plans and purposes are beyond what we can ever comprehend. When you find yourself overwhelmed with life's questions and responsibilities, you can trust in His omniscience and rest in His promises. He is faithful and His strength will never diminish.

Malachi 3:10 "Test me in this," says the LORD Almighty, "and see if I will not throw open the floodgates of heaven and pour out so much blessing that you will not have room enough for it.

Fruitful living

"Keep your servant also from willful sins; may they not rule over me. Then will I be blameless, innocent of great transgression. May the words of my mouth and the meditation of my heart be pleasing in Your sight, O LORD, my Rock and my Redeemer." (Psalm 19:13-14)

In the story of Mary and Martha (Luke 10:38-42), Jesus says that Mary chose the better way: As Jesus and his disciples were on their way, he came to a village where a woman named Martha opened her home to him. She had a sister called Mary, who sat at the Lord's feet listening to what he said. But Martha was distracted by all the preparations that had to be made.

She came to him and asked, "Lord, don't you care that my sister has left me to do the work by myself? Tell her to help me!"

"Martha, Martha," the Lord answered, "you are worried and upset about many things, but only one thing is needed. Mary has chosen what is better, and it will not be taken away from her."

Every day we make choices and decisions - each decision and the choice we make, in effect, proclaim our priorities and our commitment to holding tight to those priorities. Philippians 4:7-9 says "whatever is true, whatever is noble, whatever is right, whatever is pure, whatever is lovely, whatever is admirable - if anything is excellent or praiseworthy - think about such things."

We have so many opportunities to expose ourselves to harmful ideas, thought patterns, pictures, influences and habits. When we allow these vices to slip into our lives, we cease being fruitful for our King. We need to guard our hearts from the things that can subtly damage us from the inside out.

Jesus said in Mark 7:20, "The things that come from a person are the things that make that person wrong." As Pastor Larry always says, "The flesh dies screaming", so we need to constantly work to keep ourselves pure and learn to walk in holiness as Jesus commanded. Then we have unbroken fellowship with our Heavenly Father and His favor upon our lives, which strengthens us with joy and peace.

Proverbs 10:22 says "The blessing of the Lord makes a person rich, and He adds no sorrow with it." We need to be diligent to stop evil thoughts from entering our minds and focus on Jesus. When we obey God's command to follow Him, we are blessed by our Creator and others will notice the difference and be drawn to Him.

Matthew 6:33 says "But seek first His kingdom and His righteousness, and all these things will be given to you as well." Let's determine to submit to God's guidance, give Him first priority and learn to exemplify the life of holiness to which we've been called.

Song of Solomon 2:15 says, "Catch for us the foxes,

the little foxes that ruin the vineyards, our vineyards that are in bloom." It really is the little things in life that so easily distract us from the important things. We need to discipline ourselves and remain accountable to God for every thought, word and deed.

Endurance Produces Perfection

"Do you see what this means - all these pioneers who blazed the way, all these veterans cheering us on? It means we'd better get on with it. Strip down, start running - and never quit ! No extra spiritual fat, no parasitic sins. Keep your eyes on Jesus, who both began and finished this race we're in. Study how He did it. Because He never lost sight of where He was headed - that exhilarating finish in and with God - He could put up with anything along the way: Cross, shame, whatever. And now He's there, in the place of honor, right alongside God. When you find yourselves flagging in your faith, go over that story again, item by item, that long litany of hostility He plowed through. That will shoot adrenaline into your souls!" (Hebrews 12:1-3)

One thing I hate to do is cleaning closets! But, when we decide to clean out our closets and really get serious about living every moment of life to honor to God, He enlarges our capacity to receive. So many times, God wants to give us so much - far more than we can even imagine.

We must spend time talking to Him every day – that's how you get to know someone. He has a unique assignment for each of us. Our life is a process of "cleaning closets" - the more we commit to know the Lord with all our heart, soul and strength, the more we will see the things that need to be removed for our life to be better. Not a lot of things will remain for eternity - just as a space shuttle is heated up as it exits the atmosphere, most of the things we spend time on will be burned up when we exit this earth - and the only things remaining will be what God deems important. God doesn't look at our outward appearance, He sees our heart as it truly is; I can deceive myself at times, but God knows the real me.

So, how do we prepare for the day we stand in front of our Heavenly Father? In order to find fulfillment in this life, we need to endure whatever comes our way and maintain a heart that is completely focused on Jesus.

Hebrews 10:36 says "For you have need of steadfast patience and endurance, so that you may perform and fully accomplish the will of God, and thus receive and carry away [and enjoy to the full] what is promised." We will be content when we are living our life the way God intended, fully trusting Him along the way. Our assignment is far easier than the task required of Jesus.

G. K. Chesterton said, "Jesus promised his disciples three things - that they would be completely fearless, absurdly happy and in constant trouble." Follow Jesus' example and persevere through each trial, knowing that the reward that follows will far exceed the difficulty now. Our difficulties are temporary, but the rewards will be eternal!

Hebrews 2:9-11 says, "But we are able to see Jesus, Who was ranked lower than the angels for a little while, crowned with glory and honor because of His having suffered death, in order that by the grace (unmerited favor) of God [to us sinners] He might experience death for every individual person. For it was an act worthy [of God] and fitting [to the divine nature] that He, for Whose sake and by Whom all things have their existence, in bringing many sons into glory, should make the Pioneer of their salvation perfect [should bring to maturity the human experience necessary to be perfectly equipped for His office as High Priest] through suffering. For both He Who sanctifies [making men holy] and those who are sanctified all have one [Father]. For this reason He is not ashamed to call them brethren."

Our lives are all different, but one thing is the same: God loves us all unconditionally and He has promised to guide us along the way when we humbly submit to Him, trusting what He says. The life of Jesus reflected the character of God. If we mature and grow more like Jesus the way God intended, our life will continually grow more peaceful, joyful, loving, patient, kind, gentle, faithful and self-controlled.

With God, nothing is impossible – and if we're obedient to Him, His authority is given to us! Jesus was always doing the will of God and speaking the words of God - and that is our goal. Endurance produces perfection, but we will not reach "perfection" this side of heaven – but we can move toward that goal for an enriched life. God's Holy Spirit within us helps us to change as we obey our Creator and strive for holiness, as He is holy.

Galatians 5 and 6 tell us how to live by His Spirit, Ephesians 1 and 2 talk about having abundant life and the third chapter of Colossians gives an excellent pattern for how to live a life of holiness, drawing closer to God. Spend some time soaking in God's love letter to you. You'll never regret it!

Road Trip

"But He knows the way that I take; when He has tested me, I will come forth as gold. My feet have closely followed His steps; I have kept to His way without turning aside. I have not departed from the commands of His lips; I have treasured the words of His mouth more than my daily bread." (Job 23:10-12)

I love driving and taking long road trips - sometimes I'm almost disappointed when I reach my destination.

I think the Lord enjoys journeys, too. He loves it when we trust Him enough to "let go of the reins" and follow His guidance. Sometimes I'm curious and ask "Where are You taking me?" but in my heart He knows I am committed to following Him all the way, regardless of the ending point.

There are other times when the potholes get a little too deep, and I want to ask "Are we there yet?" Some trips seem much longer than others – especially when we cannot see where we are going. I know when I surrender my will to His guidance, He will lead the way and I will arrive in His perfect timing. That is such a relief to "let go" many times. But there are times I want to hang on and take a detour to a destination I choose on my own. He allows us to travel in our own directions at times, knowing that when we are tripped up we will return to Him, seek His forgiveness and re-orient ourselves to His plan. Proverbs 16:9 says "In his heart a man plans his course, but the

LORD determines his steps." And Proverbs 20:24 says, "A man's steps are directed by the LORD. How then can anyone understand his own way?"

I don't want to "wander aimlessly" like the Israelites in the wilderness because of their lack of trust in Him.

It's better to trust Him and follow His plan - He knows what He's doing! Jeremiah prayed "I know, O LORD, that a man's life is not his own; it is not for man to direct his steps. Correct me, LORD, but only with justice - not in Your anger, lest You reduce me to nothing. (Jeremiah 10:23-24)

"A good man is not a perfect man; a good man is an honest man, faithful and unhesitatingly responsive to the voice of God in his life." (John Fisher) Let's be unhesitatingly responsive to God's voice in our lives!

The Plan

"The king's heart is in the hand of the Lord; He directs it like a watercourse wherever He pleases. All a man's ways seem right to him, but the Lord weighs the heart." (Proverbs 21:1-2)

Wait upon God; wait for His plan to develop in your life. Remain faithful, loyal and obedient and you will see His hand at work in your life. Have you ever watched a child try to make something? They can't wait for the glue to dry so they can finish it, but they often destroy the item because of their impatience. God is patient in working with us. Stand in faith and persevere – He has a plan, and it's a good one! Soak yourself in the truths from His word – reading the bible is like reading the instructions before putting a model racecar together, or like reading your benefits manual - you will find fulfillment and abundance for your soul to feast upon, instructions for how to handle situations and benefits beyond compare! Stay away from those who seek other "gods" and prioritize the unimportant things in life. Those ways lead to leanness of soul, emptiness – forever craving but never finding fulfillment. Be content to make the Lord your focus, as only He can satisfy. Psalm 107:9 says, "For He satisfies the longing soul and fills the hungry soul with good."

God is the author and perfecter of our faith – He created us and He designed us to find contentment in a relationship with Him! It's built-in and nothing else will satisfy. His plan will stand forever, so seek Him for direction and lift up those in leadership, trusting that God is bringing about His plan through your prayers.

(Psalm 33:9-11) "For He spoke, and it was done; He commanded, and it stood fast. The Lord nullifies the counsel of the nations; He frustrates the plans of the peoples. The counsel of the Lord stands forever - the plans of His heart from generation to generation."

God's desire is for our success – He is more interested in our character than our comfort! Let Him lead you through the situations on this earth and trust that He is designing you for something more important. His ways are greater than we can understand and His plans are beyond our ability to see. Trust Him to deliver you from every scheme of the enemy. Psalm 138:7-8 says, "Though I walk in the midst of trouble, You preserve my life; You stretch out Your hand against the anger of my foes, with Your right hand You save me. The Lord will fulfill His purpose for me. Your love, Lord, endures forever - do not abandon the works of Your hands."

God is just and His love for us far exceeds our love for anything. He cannot help Himself, He thinks of us continually because of His love for us. When you make something and spend lots of time perfecting the final product, you think about it frequently throughout the building process. You take pride in it - making sure it is done right. Projects made with excellence are highly valued and you want yours to last. That's how God is with us: (Psalm 105:8) "He is [earnestly] mindful of His covenant and forever it is imprinted on His heart, the word which He commanded and established to a thousand generations."

God is always thinking about us and aware of the motive of our hearts. When we cry out to Him for help, desiring to be in right standing with Him, He is always faithful to help us. We need to share these experiences with others and show them what an authentic relationship with our Heavenly Father looks like and how He blesses us when we have a dynamic friendship with our Creator. Spend time thanking God for what He has done and is doing – and tell others about His great power in helping you through life's bumps along the journey. Psalm 107:19 says, "Then they cry to the Lord in their trouble, and He delivers them out of their distresses. He sends forth His word and heals them; He rescues them from the pit and destruction. Oh, that men would praise [and confess to] the Lord for His goodness and loving-kindness and His wonderful works to the children of men!"

In moments of joy
all of us wish we possessed
a tail we could wag.

Let Your Spirit Rule

"I don't know about you, but I'm running hard for the finish line. I'm giving it everything I've got. No sloppy living for me! I'm staying alert and in top condition. I'm not going to get caught napping, telling everyone else all about it and then missing out myself." (I Corinthians 9:26-27)

Studying the bible makes me appreciate God's grace so much more – I am so thankful I did not live in biblical times! I'd have been stoned to death on many occasions for my behavior. Thinking about God's desire to have a holy people, separate unto Himself, purging sinfulness from the society and people that He loved makes me realize how awesome His forgiveness is toward me. I cannot really comprehend how far-reaching and all-embracing His mercy really is, but I am forever grateful. It compels me to be more diligent in making sure my thoughts, words and deeds do not grieve God's precious Holy Spirit. We cannot fully understand all that He has done for us – but the stories in the bible reveal the seriousness of God when He says, "I am the Lord your God who brought you out of Egypt – be holy, for I am holy." (Lev 22:31-33) and in Isaiah 48:17: "Thus says the LORD, your Redeemer, the Holy One of Israel, 'I am the LORD your God, who teaches you to profit, who leads you in the way you should go.'"

The activities we see in today's society desensitize us

to what the word "holy" actually means. As we mature in Christ, and live in continuous communion with God throughout our day, we learn to go about doing His will more and more naturally. Initially, it takes a lot of effort on our part to make our body submit to God's spirit within us in every area, purging out the wrongs within us; they all start in our thoughts and lead to our influence, character and reputation. As Sally Nguyen stated, "Faith makes it possible, not easy." It's a daily effort, a moment by moment focus and an intentional mindset to which we commit. It requires renewing our mind on a regular basis, spending time throughout each day relating to our Heavenly Father. From these times with God, we set our priorities from a long list of things that seem important.

It is easy to deceive ourselves, compare ourselves with others and say "I'm doing my best" or "I'm only human".

But when we look into God's truth, we are faced with a higher standard – and it is by His power that we reach that standard! Philippians 2:12-13 says, "So then, My dear friends, just as you have always obeyed, not only in My presence, but now even more in My absence, work out your own salvation with fear and trembling; for it is God who is working in you, enabling you both to will and to act for His good purpose."

The more we practice living by God's spirit within us, the more we will strengthen our spirit life over our flesh (carnal nature). And it does get easier as the life of Christ gets stronger within us. Fasting is an excellent example – but our goal cannot be what we will gain. Our purpose must be to know God more intimately, hear His voice more clearly and respond more quickly. God desires to have disciples that represent Him in the earth – to draw others to Him by the light that He gives us to shine to those around us. If we are no different than those who do not believe, how can we stand out? Our actions need to align with God's Words to us – and that is in direct conflict with life in this world. We are a peculiar people because we go against the flow of society.

We are called to minister to others the way Jesus did when He walked the earth – we have the strength given to us by His Spirit continually. We cannot minister to others when we have polluted waters flowing within us. Take time to meditate on the words that flow from you – are they positive, faith-building and encouraging to others? Do they point to your wholehearted love, devotion and trust in God Almighty, Creator of heaven and earth? Do they show the closeness of your relationship with your holy Heavenly Father throughout your day? Or do you speak what you see with your eyes, as the world does?

There is another realm that we need to be in-tune with. When you tune an instrument, you don't use other instruments, you use a tuning fork so all the instruments are tuned to the same key. We don't tune our lives with the lives of those around us – only with Jesus – He is our "tuning fork" so when the body of Christ gathers together, we all reflect Him in perfect unity. God created heaven and earth – surely we can trust Him with our problems!

He gives us the wisdom we need to live our life according to the purposes He chose for us before we were born.

II Corinthians 9: 8-11 says, "God can pour on the blessings in astonishing ways so that you're ready for anything and everything, more than just ready to do what needs to be done. As one psalmist puts it, 'He throws caution to the winds, giving to the needy in reckless abandon. His right-living, right-giving ways never run out, never wear out.' This most generous God who gives seed to the farmer that becomes bread for your meals is more than extravagant with you. He gives you something you can then give away, which grows into full-formed lives, robust in God, wealthy in every way, so that you can be generous in every way, producing with us great praise to God." and Psalm 138:8 says, "The Lord will perfect that which concerns me; Your mercy and loving-kindness, O Lord, endure forever - forsake not the works of Your own hands."

Peculiar People

"But you are the ones chosen by God, chosen for the high calling of priestly work, chosen to be a holy people, God's instruments to do His work and speak out for Him, to tell others of the night-and-day difference He made for you - from nothing to something, from rejected to accepted. Friends, this world is not your home, so don't make yourselves cozy in it. Don't indulge your ego at the expense of your soul. Live an exemplary life among the natives so that your actions will refute their prejudices. Then they'll be won over to God's side and be there to join in the celebration when He arrives." (1 Peter 2:9-12)

Whatever we do, we are to do with excellence since we represent the King of Kings, the Creator of the world! We claim to be His children, so we need to resemble Him more and more as we grow up. As a dearly loved child imitates his or her father, so should we try to be more like Christ in everything we say and do – and that begins with every thought we entertain.

We have many opportunities to set an example, and many times we forget that we are sending a message – in a quick phone call, as we pass an acquaintance in the store or parking lot, the e-mails we send.

Everything we say and do is proclaiming something to those around us, whether they are Christians or not. Think twice before speaking that word in haste or developing an attitude. Read your e-mails before you send them to make sure they are worthy of representing a "King's kid" – that's who you are! Would you send it to Jesus?

Don't grieve His Spirit within you. I know sometimes I am too flippant in my knee-jerk reactions to things I see and experience around me – and at times there would not be sufficient evidence to prove I was a Christians if I sat down in court to defend myself. We all need to continually work on these things in our lives.

I need to remember that I am called to a life of holiness for a reason – it isn't meant to make life miserable while here on earth. God's plan is that, as we become like Him, He will be lifted up, and others will be drawn to Him.

If we say one thing and live another, there is no credibility and no one will want to follow us or the one we claim to live for: Jesus. That is why we need a daily diet of reading God's word – it is the opposite of what our culture looks like.

In order to reflect God and not the world, we need to spend more time with God than elsewhere, and get more heavenly-minded to know God's heart and share in His compassion for the lost.

1 Peter 2:1-3 says, "So be done with every trace of wickedness and all deceit and insincerity (pretense, hypocrisy) and grudges (envy, jealousy) and slander and evil speaking of every kind. Like newborn babies you should crave (thirst for, earnestly desire) the pure (unadulterated) spiritual milk, that by it you may be nurtured and grow unto [completed] salvation, since you have [already] tasted the goodness and kindness of the Lord."

Rise Up: "The Hot Air Balloon Experience"

"His divine power has given us everything we need for life and godliness through our knowledge of him who called us by his own glory and goodness. Through these he has given us his very great and precious promises, so that through them you may participate in the divine nature and escape the corruption in the world caused by evil desires. For this very reason, make every effort to add to your faith goodness; and to goodness, knowledge; and to knowledge, self-control; and to self-control, perseverance; and to perseverance, godliness; and to godliness, brotherly kindness; and to brotherly kindness, love. For if you possess these qualities in increasing measure, they will keep you from being ineffective and unproductive in your knowledge of our Lord Jesus Christ." (II Peter 1:3-8)

Everyone faces times of weariness when we lack the energy required to "seek God first". Many times it is a struggle to fight the tendency to become lazy and to let our habits get out of control. Seeking God only on Sunday is not enough to walk in God's victory – we must discipline ourselves daily to take in scriptures from the bible and spend time speaking and listening to God's still, quiet voice. Only then can we steady our feet and align them with the path God has before us.

He longs to speak to each one of us, individually – and not always through other people. We all have a unique opportunity to commune with God and hear Him speak to us, specifically. And He, in return, longs to hear each of us speak from our heart to Him. Our times spent seeking God are for our own benefit. Job 33:26 says "He prays to God and finds favor with Him, he sees God's face and shouts for joy; he is restored by God to his righteous state."

Our lives are like hot air balloons – just as a hot air balloon needs that fire to release hot air to go up, we need to feed ourselves with spiritual "manna" to continually "rise up". Second Timothy says, "That is why I would remind you to stir up (rekindle the embers of, fan the flame of, and keep burning) the [gracious] gift of God, [the inner fire] that is in you by means of the laying on of my hands... For God did not give us a spirit of timidity (of cowardice, of craven and cringing and fawning fear), but [He has given us a spirit] of power and of love and of calm and well-balanced mind and discipline and self-control."

As soon as we neglect meeting with God and talking to Him each day, we immediately begin our descent. Continually mark your progress toward becoming more Christlike to avoid falling into the trap of deceit, where the enemy likes us to think we're "good enough" and let go of the reigns a bit – and refuse to compare yourself to others. The nature of our flesh is to please our self – but we know that only leads to ruin. First Corinthians 15:58 says, "Therefore, be steadfast, immovable, always abounding in the work of the Lord, knowing that your toil is not in vain in the Lord."

Thank God that He has placed His spirit within us, so we do not need to rely on will power alone. Psalms 139 tells us we cannot escape His presence, and He continues to pursue us for our own good. Rest in Him and take time to listen to Him for direction - Psalm 12:6 says "And the words of the LORD are flawless, like silver refined in a furnace of clay, purified seven times." Do not run from Him, but run toward Him – and see the good He has in store!

Chapter Five – WORSHIP

Live Generously

"Jesus sent His twelve harvest hands out with this charge: 'Don't begin by traveling to some far-off place to convert unbelievers. And don't try to be dramatic by tackling some public enemy. Go to the lost, confused people right here in the neighborhood. Tell them that the kingdom is here. Bring health to the sick. Raise the dead. Touch the untouchables. Kick out the demons. You have been treated generously, so live generously. Don't think you have to put on a fund-raising campaign before you start. You don't need a lot of equipment. You are the equipment, and all you need to keep that going is three meals a day. Travel light.'" (Matt 10:5-10)

The key to living well is giving generously. Just take a look at nature: a kernel of corn yields a plant full of corn cobs containing hundreds of kernels. Every plant, tree – and even weeds – give up numerous seeds to multiply their kind. The sun, stars and moon give light. Everything God created has within its nature a giving quality – so how generous should we be for all we have received from Him! Don't give your used tea bags to the missionaries – send a lavish gift, even if you must sacrifice in order to give it. Do your best deed for others. Give gifts of excellence – not to earn favor, but because your gifts represent who you are – and we are heirs of God and co-heirs with Christ.

I read a story once about two different seas in Palestine. One of them receives streams from the Jordan River, and it continues to flow, remaining a fresh body of water and allowing plants, fish and birds to live in and around it. The other one is the Dead Sea, whose shoreline is said to be the lowest point of dry land on earth, approximately 1300 feet below sea level. It receives streams from the Jordan River, but does not continue to flow, so the water evaporates, leaving just minerals behind, thus becoming more salty each day. There is no outlet, just stagnant water – therefore no life exists within it or in the surrounding area. The analogy seen here is true everywhere: fulfillment in life is found in giving! Second Corinthians 8:7 says, "But just as you excel in everything – in faith, in speech, in knowledge, in complete earnestness and in your love for us – see that you also excel in this grace of giving."

The secret to "The Good Life"

"Your life is a journey you must travel with a deep consciousness of God. It cost God plenty to get you out of that dead-end, empty-headed life you grew up in. He paid with Christ's sacred blood, you know. He died like an unblemished, sacrificial lamb. And this was no afterthought. Even though it has only lately—at the end of the ages—become public knowledge, God always knew he was going to do this for you. It's because of this sacrificed Messiah, whom God then raised from the dead and glorified, that you trust God, that you know you have a future in God." (I Peter 18-21)

Sometimes I think we try to make "the good life" more complicated than it really is – which is why many people run when they hear the word "Christian" or "salvation". It may take a lifetime to become all that we want to, but it's the journey that makes up life. Simplify your life and look at each decision as a step that determines your journey's success. The One who created you knows what your life should look like – you were created for greatness! The only thing hindering that level of success is when we make ourselves an idol and lean toward selfishness – that one thing, wanting it all to be about me, is called "sin". But turn it around and focus on your Creator, trusting Him to lead you, and that is called "worship". Below are two quotes which I then simplify to make them easier to apply in life.

Here is a definition of sin by Susanna Wesley in a letter written June 8, 1725 ~ "Take this rule: whatever weakens your reason, impairs the tenderness of your conscience, obscures your sense of God, or takes off your relish of spiritual things; in short, whatever increases the strength and authority of your body over your mind, that thing is sin to you, however innocent it may be in itself."

Here's a quote about worship by William Temple:

"Worship is the submission of all our nature to God. It is the quickening of the conscience by His holiness; the nourishment of mind with His truth; the purifying of the imagination by His beauty; the opening of the heart to His love; the surrender of will to His purpose - and all of this gathered up in adoration, the most selfless emotion of which our nature is capable, and therefore the chief remedy of that self-centeredness which is our original sin and the source of all actual sin."

Tying these two quotes together and simplifying them a bit makes it easier for me to apply to life and see what I need to do to follow the plan of my Creator for my life. Worship is difficult for us because of our innate tendency to focus on our self, so when I commit to worshipping God I have to take the following actions:

– to submit all my behavior/temperament to God;
- to stimulate my conscience by His perfect holiness;
- to feed and strengthen my mind with His truth;
- to filter my imagination by His beauty, freeing it by removing harmful, inferior thoughts;

- to open my heart to His unconditional love and reflect that love to others;
- to relinquish total control of my will to His purpose – and to adore Him with unhindered emotion and complete selflessness – maintaining Him alone as my focus.

The more we practice this, the more it will become part of who we are. Worship is to be a continual activity in our daily walk through this life.

Our Thoughts

"We demolish arguments and every pretension that sets itself up against the knowledge of God, and we take captive every thought to make it obedient to Christ." (II Corinthians 10:5)

Our thoughts become our actions. We need to make a "Detour" sign in our mind to "take captive every thought to make it obedient to Christ". "The Message" version of II Corinthians 10:5 says we use the gifts God has given us to smash warped philosophies, tear down walls built against the truth of God, fitting every loose thought and emotion and impulse into the structure of life shaped by Christ. Our gifts are like tools ready at hand for clearing the ground of every obstruction and building lives of obedience into maturity.

Every decision we make matters for eternity: our own eternity and the eternity of those we influence. Sometimes we are not aware of who we influence, so we need to watch our every move and the motives of our heart. When we are obedient, God will bless us and use us to bless those around us. First Corinthians 2:9 says: "Eye has not seen, nor ear heard, nor have entered into the heart of man the things which God has prepared for those who love Him." We need to take everything in our life and place it in the plan God made and keeps ready for us, as we hold Him in affectionate reverence. We need to obey Him and gratefully recognize the benefits He gives us. Let's set aside time to worship Him with awe today. The fear of God is the beginning of knowledge. To fear God is to have respect and reverence for God and to be in awe of his majesty and power. This is the starting point to finding real wisdom – and when we shun evil, we will gain understanding (Job 28:28).

Engage Your Spirit

"But he knows where I am and what I've done. He can cross-examine me all he wants, and I'll pass the test with honors. I've followed him closely, my feet in his footprints, not once swerving from his way. I've obeyed every word he's spoken, and not just obeyed his advice - I've treasured it." (Job 23:10-12)

Worshipping God sometimes reminds me of the story of the Prodigal. Breaking the story down into a simple word picture, here are the twelve steps that the Prodigal Son took: 1. "Give me", 2. He gathered, 3. He journeyed, 4. He squandered, 5. He became impoverished, 6. He worked, 7. He wanted, 8. He came to his senses, 9. He planned, 10. He humbly returned (and was well received), 11. He repented, and 12. Everyone celebrated!

How easy for me to point to several of those steps in my journey! I love the part: "when he came to his senses"; he thought about his situation, planned to return to his father, humbly confessed of his wrong-doing, asking forgiveness and to serve with his father's slaves. He returned to his father, "pig smell and all" – we need to do that, more often and more quickly. When we worship God, we expose our "pig-smelly-selves" to the unconditional love of our Heavenly Father. We receive His redeeming grace, becoming clothed in the robe of righteousness.

John 4:23-24 says "It's who you are and the way you

live that counts before God. Your worship must engage your spirit in the pursuit of truth. That's the kind of people the Father is out looking for: those who are simply and honestly themselves before Him in their worship. God is sheer being itself – Spirit. Those who worship Him must do it out of their very being, their spirits, their true selves, in adoration." I think when the Prodigal Son came to his senses, he began the process of "engaging his spirit"- that's not just something that happens spontaneously. We have to work toward that – but it certainly is well worth the effort!

We freely make ourselves vulnerable to our Heavenly Father because we know we can trust Him. I recently read that "worship is like a two-way conversation, unpredictable and open-ended" (Unquenchable Worshipper, by Matt Redman). When we open up in worship and share our heart, He works in us and through us, tearing down strongholds. He knows everything about us, so we might as well be real before Him – we can't fake reality. And He is not going to condemn us when we approach Him with reckless abandon. When our heart is right, He will embrace us – and nothing heals like God's embrace! Soak it in and worship Him with everything that's in you.

Psalm 139:1-24 ~ GOD, investigate my life; get all the facts firsthand. I'm an open book to you; even from a distance, you know what I'm thinking. You know when I leave and when I get back; I'm never out of your sight. You know everything I'm going to say before I start the first sentence. I look behind me and you're there, then up ahead and you're there, too - your reassuring presence, coming and going. This is too much, too wonderful - I can't take it all in! Is there anyplace I can go to avoid your Spirit? To be out of your sight? If I climb to the sky, you're there! If I go underground, you're there! If I flew on morning's wings to the far western horizon, You'd find me in a minute - you're already there waiting! Then I said to myself, "Oh, he even sees me in the dark! At night I'm immersed in the light!" It's a fact: darkness isn't dark to you; night and day, darkness and light, they're all the same to you.

Oh yes, you shaped me first inside, then out; you formed me in my mother's womb. I thank you, High God - you're breathtaking! Body and soul, I am marvelously made! I worship in adoration - what a creation! You know me inside and out, you know every bone in my body; You know exactly how I was made, bit by bit, how I was sculpted from nothing into something.

Like an open book, you watched me grow from conception to birth; all the stages of my life were spread out before you, the days of my life all prepared before I'd even lived one day. Your thoughts - how rare, how beautiful! God, I'll never comprehend them! I couldn't even begin to count them - any more than I could count the sand of the sea. Oh, let me rise in the morning and live always with you! And please, God, do away with wickedness for good! And you murderers - out of here! - all the men and women who belittle you, God, infatuated with cheap god-imitations. See how I hate those who hate you, God, see how I loathe all this godless arrogance; I hate it with pure, unadulterated hatred. Your enemies are my enemies!

Investigate my life, O God, find out everything about me; Cross-examine and test me, get a clear picture of what I'm about; See for yourself whether I've done anything wrong - then guide me on the road to eternal life.

Extravagant Gratitude

"Do you see what we've got? An unshakable kingdom! And do you see how thankful we must be? Not only thankful, but brimming with worship, deeply reverent before God." (Hebrews 12:28-29)

Thanksgiving and worship go hand-in-hand. When we give thanks to God for all that He has done, we have taken the first step in worship!

First, we acknowledge that it is God who has done great things in our lives, from the very creation of this planet we live on to weaving together our innermost parts (Psalm 139). He knows everything about us and He still loves us! We love Him because He first loved us – and if we are wise, we commit to following Him by faith, obeying what He has told us in the bible and what He continues to speak to our hearts each day.

Knowing that He is in control of everything, we are free to "let go" of everything! What a liberating thought! He loves us more than we can imagine, His love endures forever. There is nothing we can do to separate ourselves from His love, and He is blazing a trail ahead of us so we will know where to turn and what to do as we continue to trust His leading!

Psalm 100:3-5 says: "Know that the LORD is God. It is He who made us, and we are His; we are his people, the sheep of His pasture. Enter His gates with thanksgiving and His courts with praise; give thanks to Him and praise His name. For the LORD is good and His love endures forever; His faithfulness continues through all generations."

When we thank Jesus and really focus on all He has done for us, we cannot contain the joy the rises up within us. God is all-powerful and He's our King, our "Daddy" and our friend! Nothing should move us when we keep our focus on Him. Let's encourage one another with the great news about who God is and how much He loves us, and spend time worshipping Him for all that He has done and all that He is going to do!

I Chronicles 16:26-30 ~ "Sing to GOD, everyone and everything! Get out His salvation news every day! Publish His glory among the godless nations, His wonders to all races and religions. And why?

Because GOD is great - well worth praising! No god or goddess comes close in honor. All the popular gods are stuff and nonsense, but GOD made the cosmos!

Splendor and majesty flow out of Him, strength and joy fill His place. Shout Bravo! To God, families of the peoples, in awe of the Glory, in awe of the Strength: Bravo! Shout Bravo! To His famous Name, lift high an offering and enter His presence! Stand resplendent in His robes of holiness!

God is serious business, take Him seriously. He's put the earth in place and it's not moving. So let Heaven rejoice, let Earth be jubilant, and pass the word among the nations, "GOD reigns!"

Let Ocean, all teeming with life, bellow, let Field

and all its creatures shake the rafters; Then the trees in the forest will add their applause to all who are pleased and present before GOD - He's on His way to set things right!"

No More Toil

"For the eyes of the Lord range throughout the earth to strengthen those whose hearts are fully committed to Him." (II Chronicles 16:9)

When life gets busy and we become weary, it is easy to forget that we are redeemed from the curse – therefore we "toil no more"! Do not be distracted by life's busyness and become worn out by things that have no eternal value. We need to remember to keep our focus on Jesus because there is purpose and strength in our relationship with Him. Continually return to Him, making Him your first priority, and also find your rest in Him. John 15 says Jesus is the true vine and our Heavenly Father is the gardener:

"Remain in Me and I will remain in you. No branch can bear fruit by itself; it must remain in the vine. Neither can you bear fruit unless you remain in Me. I am the vine; you are the branches. If a man remains in Me, he will bear much fruit; apart from Me you can do nothing." (John 15:4-5)

Just like grapes becoming raisins, we lose our strength so quickly when we are cut off from the vine. Romans 12:11 exhorts us to "Never be lacking in zeal, but keep your spiritual fervor, serving the Lord." When we keep our focus on Him we are rejuvenated by the power of the Holy Spirit. Luke 11:13 says, "If you then, evil as you are, know how to give good gifts [gifts that are to their advantage] to your children, how much more will your heavenly Father give the Holy Spirit to those who ask and continue to ask Him!"

We're called to a purpose far beyond what we consider ourselves capable of living - and God promises to provide the strength necessary to fulfill our destiny. He is more concerned about our relationship with Him and our character than what we do for Him.

We represent the King – think about that! If America was ruled by a king today and we knew we could have a close relationship with him, we would not hesitate to develop that relationship as well as share our thoughts and ideas with him, listen to what he had to say, serve him, work with excellence, say kind things, think about our deeds and hope to obtain his favor! The same should be true of our desire to know our Heavenly Father more.

Our lives are to be a sacrifice to the Creator of the Universe - He gave us His only Son while we were still stained with wrongdoing. We cannot out-give God! When you give away your time, talents, and gifts – do so with a good attitude, unto the Lord - and know that God will return that to you in good measure.

Eternal rewards are gained when we wholeheartedly give to the Lord without grumbling and complaining.

Eternal souls will profit when we are obedient to our Heavenly Father. And He promises that His yoke is easy and His burden is light. We have no room for shrinking back from the task He has called us to.

John 12:24 says "Listen carefully: Unless a grain of wheat is buried in the ground, dead to the world, it is never any more than a grain of wheat. But if it is buried, it sprouts and reproduces itself many times over. In the same way, anyone who holds on to life just as it is destroys that life. But if you let it go, reckless in your love, you'll have it forever, real and eternal.

Give Thanks

"Through God then, let us continually offer up a sacrifice of praise to God that is the fruit of lips that give thanks to His name. And do not neglect doing good and sharing; for with such sacrifices God is pleased." (Hebrews 13:15-16)

I remember as a child, whenever we'd celebrate "Mother's Day" and I would ask "When is it 'children's day'", Mom's quick answer would be "EVERYDAY is 'children's day'!" Well, I'm not sure if that's true, but I do think everyday should be Thanksgiving Day! We so often neglect to offer words of thanks or gratitude from our hearts, when we are so indebted to so many who deserve to hear those words. I like the John Maxwell's quote, "As soon as we are born we are indebted to our mother for nine months' room and board."

When I was 17 I got my first vehicle. I was so excited to have my own vehicle finally, instead of borrowing one. It was late in December when I picked it up on a Friday and by Monday morning it was in the ditch. I was on my way to school and the roads were really icy. Since it was a five speed, I pushed in the clutch when I noticed it sliding, but it continued to skid sideways and head for the deep ditch. Thankfully, a small tree caught the front corner of the little truck half way down and it didn't go all the way into the ditch. I was surprisingly calm, since I knew I had done nothing wrong (for once), and the song I had learned at church popped into my head: "Break forth into joy, oh my soul". I thought that was strange, but I made myself sing that song as I walked back home, and my confidence that God would take care of everything soared the more I sang. I prayed that God would work out the details of this incident for whatever purpose He had in mind. In the end, it all worked out - my brother came and pulled the truck out of the ditch. There were no dents or scratches on it and we fixed the sticky emergency brake that caused the skidding. I was once again happy to have my vehicle, thankful for my brother, and smarter from that experience. First Thessalonians 5:16-18 says, "Always be joyful. Always keep on praying. No matter what happens, always be thankful, for this is God's will for you who belong to Christ Jesus."

I think God is pleased when we look past the situations we face and commit to putting our faith in Him, no matter what the circumstances look like. Isaiah 25:1 says, "O Lord, You are my God; I will exalt You and praise Your name, for in perfect faithfulness You have done marvelous things, things planned long ago." We need to remember the great things God has done for us and continually give thanks for His commitment to always be with us.

Colossians 2:6 - 7 says, "Just as you received Christ Jesus as Lord, continue to live in Him, rooted and built up in Him, strengthened in the faith as you were taught, and overflowing with thankfulness." It is God who is always with us and from whom we receive every good and perfect gift. When we choose to give Him thanks, we are choosing to take our eyes off our self and focus on Him - it isn't always easy... selfishness grows. The Israelites prove that grumbling and complaining is easier. Even when they received manna from heaven, they continued to dwell on their own expectations, monotony and boredom - because of the selfishness that filled their hearts. Being thankful proves that our hearts are right with God, we are aware of His provision and we are appreciative for the gifts He blesses us with. "The person who has stopped being thankful has fallen asleep in life." -- Robert Louis Stevenson

In America, we celebrate Thanksgiving because our earliest ancestors considered it important for this entire nation to set aside time to give thanks to God.

Written in 1782, one of the first declarations concerning the day of Thanksgiving reads: "The United States in Congress assembled, taking into their consideration the many instances of divine goodness to these States: ... Do hereby recommend to the inhabitants of these States in general, the observation of THURSDAY the twenty-eight day of NOVEMBER next, as a day of solemn THANKSGIVING to GOD for all his mercies: and they do further recommend to all ranks, to testify to their gratitude to GOD for his goodness, by a cheerful obedience of his laws, and by promoting, each in his station, and by his influence, the practice of true and undefiled religion, which is the great foundation of public prosperity and national happiness." Thanksgiving Proclamation State of New-Hampshire. In Committee of Safety, Exeter, November 1, 1782 from https://www.history.com.

Not of this world

"We have this kind of confidence toward God through Christ: not that we are competent in ourselves to consider anything as coming from ourselves, but our competence is from God." (II Corinthians 3:4-5)

Trying to think of New Year's resolutions sometimes feels overwhelming to me… especially in light of the looming memories from last year's resolutions that never came to fruition. In my mind, according to my own abilities, it seems futile to set high standards for the coming year, knowing the statistics of those who actually follow through with resolutions and realizing my lack of self-discipline at times.

Second Corinthians 12:9 encourages us, "But He {God} said to me, 'My grace is sufficient for you, for My power is perfected in weakness.'" I really need to focus on setting the highest standard I know, because God's plan is far greater than anything I can imagine. If I am trusting in His strength, then nothing is impossible for me! God will be my provision, so I focus on the unseen and try to see God's plan for my life with eternity in mind – that's faith! Micah 6:8 says, "He has told you men what is good and what it is the Lord requires of you: Only to act justly, to love faithfulness, and to walk humbly with your God."

So, when I hear the news on the television, I can be thankful that my citizenship is of another kingdom – I am not of this world. Bad news predicting a dismal future is of no concern for me – my God shall supply all my needs. So while I am in this world, I will obey God's commands and trust that He will take care of me, far beyond what I ever imagined! Proverbs 16:20 says, "Whoever gives heed to instruction prospers, and blessed is he who trusts in the Lord."

So that is my motivation to set high standards for myself. Whatever I do, I want to do it with excellence to please God and give Him glory for all that He has done for me. When I look at my past and see all the failures, or even look at my hopes to get out of those pits I dug myself into, I can clearly see that God far exceeded my wildest expectations and lifted me above and beyond anything I could have imagined! His plan all along was to prosper me; He was just waiting for me to be obedient! And His word is true – when we are obedient, He is faithful to bless us. So my goal becomes to "Love the Lord *my* God with all *my* heart and with all *my* soul and with all *my* mind and with all *my* strength." (Mark 12:30) and "He must become greater, I must become less." (John 3:30)

Second Corinthians 4:7 says "Now we have this treasure in clay jars, so that this extraordinary power may be from God and not from us." When we put our focus on Him, and long to obey His Word to us and please Him with our actions, goals, dreams and visions, we can be sure that He stands alongside us to guide our every move, thought and plan. We cannot fail and we cannot set our sights too high. God gives us our heart's desires – He

166

puts the desire in our heart and then helps us succeed to achieve those things. There is no room for fear when we know that He promises to make us victorious! He knows the end from the beginning and He has already won! With God on our side, it is ridiculous to ever have any doubt!

True Worship

"Hallelujah! Thank God! And why? Because He's good, because His love lasts. But who on earth can do it - declaim God's mighty acts, broadcast all His praises? You're one happy man when you do what's right, one happy woman when you form the habit of justice." (Psalm 106:1-3)

Many times when I try to worship, my attention span seems to drop to five second intervals. I fight it and try to concentrate on really worshipping, and it takes several attempts to really focus on truly worshipping my Lord and Savior.

True worship means being totally and wholly submitted to God – when everything within me is consumed with and wrapped up in focusing on who God is, what He has done for me and for all of creation, His love for me and how much I love Him and want to be like Him.

When I played pool, I would become so focused on the game that nothing else entered into my thinking; I couldn't hear conversations taking place around me. I was "in the zone" and because of that focus and complete concentration, I was at my best.

That is how we need to focus our attention in worshipping God on a regular basis. If we wait for Sunday morning to arrive to fix our thoughts on Him, we will never have the attention span necessary. This focus requires a daily "practice" of focusing your attention on God.

William Temple once said this about worship: "It is the quickening of the conscience by His holiness; the nourishment of mind with His truth; the purifying of imagination by His beauty; the opening of the heart to His love; the surrender of will to His purpose – all this gathered up in adoration, the most selfless emotion of which our nature is capable."

We need to "wean" ourselves from the thoughts that arise from living in this world and focus on life in the spiritual realm – try to think like God thinks. Focus on things in eternity and imagine yourself looking into God's eyes, embracing Him and having a heart to heart conversation with Him. When you can do that, everything little concern will fade away.

Psalm 111: 1-10 ~ "Hallelujah! I give thanks to God with everything I've got - Wherever good people gather, and in the congregation. God's works are so great, worth a lifetime of study - endless enjoyment! Splendor and beauty mark His craft; His generosity never gives out. His miracles are his memorial - This God of Grace, this God of Love. He gave food to those who fear Him, He remembered to keep His ancient promise. He proved to his people that He could do what He said: Hand them the nations on a platter—a gift! He manufactures truth and justice; All His products are guaranteed to last - Never out-of-date, never obsolete, rust-proof. All that He makes and does is honest and true: He paid the ransom for His people, He ordered His Covenant kept forever. He's so personal and holy, worthy of our respect. The good life begins in the fear of God - Do that and you'll know the blessing of God. His Hallelujah lasts forever!"

Chapter Six – PRAYER

Find Me

"What do you think? If a man has a hundred sheep, and one of them has gone astray and gets lost, will he not leave the ninety-nine on the mountain and go in search of the one that is lost? And if it should be that he finds it, truly I say to you, he rejoices more over it than over the ninety-nine that did not get lost. Just so it is not the will of My Father Who is in heaven that one of these little ones should be lost and perish." (Matthew 18:12-14)

I was in Meijer the other night and passed a father with two sons in the toys aisle. One son was so little he rode in the cart and the other boy was probably about 4 or 5 years old, walking alongside his dad. As I continued down the aisles, they stood there looking at a something specific the boys obviously liked. About five minutes later I was several aisles down and I heard the son calling to his dad as he was walking – his voice getting louder and louder. Finally, he became frantic and was screaming, "Daddy, please find me!" over and over as his voice went past my aisle and continued throughout the store until I couldn't hear it any longer. About 5 minutes later, I heard his dad calling out his son's name – apparently he hadn't heard the child calling to him earlier. His voice

171

got more and more anxious as he continued throughout the store calling to his son. At that point, I felt really bad that I hadn't intervened – apparently, I don't have the heart of a parent. I just assumed the little boy had found his dad. But I remember thinking of the words the little boy used: Daddy, please find me! That really affected me because many times I have cried out to my Heavenly Father, "Please find me, please draw me back to You, please help me." Even though the state of being lost is entirely my own fault, I cry out to Him to lead me back to Himself. And He is always faithful to do so, but in the meantime, since it's not usually an immediate experience, I have time to think about what caused the distance to begin with. We may not intentionally leave our Father's side, but eventually we learn that the decisions we make separate us from our Heavenly Father. Since God is a holy God, the God of justice, He cannot bless us when we choose to do things that are not in line with His direction. But when we "come to our senses", because He is a merciful God, He will show us the way back into that close communication with Him so we can be protected again, like a hen gathers her chicks under her wings. We are never separated from His love for us.

The Bellamy Brothers sing a song that reminds me of how I feel when I have distanced myself from God: When I'm away from you, I can't stay still. My thoughts won't move from the way I feel. It happens time and time again, and the circle never ends. Another verse says: When I'm away from you... My sense has gone, I'm up all through the night, and I can't tell wrong from right… It's all the things you do that make life worthwhile. It's a love song and it applies to almost every relationship, when we lose someone we love – or like the Prodigal Son, when we've wandered away from our Father. It is my Heavenly Father who makes my life worthwhile, and when I'm separated from that closeness with Him, I can't sleep at night, I can't tell wrong from right and I know something important is missing from my life. I am so thankful that God is always faithful to help me return to Him – every time.

Psalm 119:175-176 says, "Let me live that I may praise you, and may your laws sustain me. I have strayed like a lost sheep. Seek your servant, for I have not forgotten your commands."

Close the Gap

"The Pharisees and religious scholars asked, 'Why do your disciples flout the rules, showing up at meals without washing their hands?' Jesus answered, 'Isaiah was right about frauds like you, hit the bull's-eye in fact: These people make a big show of saying the right thing, but their heart isn't in it. They act like they are worshiping Me, but they don't mean it. They just use Me as a cover for teaching whatever suits their fancy, ditching God's command and taking up the latest fads.'" (Mark 7:5-7)

I have to remind myself that it is only because of Jesus – and the personal relationship I have with Him and God's people – that I even understand anything about truth, abundant life and eternity – which are the things that really matter. My natural mind cannot comprehend how great God is without living by faith and developing a two-way relationship with the Jesus. So many times my mind wants to take me to the "proverbial pigpen", thinking I can quickly visit and then find my way out – but as the song suggests, "it's a slow fade". Allowing ourselves a quick glance or thought in the wrong direction will surely end up leading us into deceit; and sin will always be exposed eventually. Following the latest trends and doing what everybody else is doing is not always harmless – it deviates from the road God has intended we follow – and only His path will lead us to being holy, as He is holy. And only a relationship with Him will guide us into abundant life, because of His infinite wisdom. I cannot see the big picture to know how or where to navigate – my limited mind perceives what is seen. So I have to trust God for what I cannot see. To the very detail that I take His holiness seriously is the same level that He will lead me to becoming more like Him. If I only pay attention to the big stuff, then the gap between my Heavenly Father and myself remains a huge chasm. But when I thoroughly and diligently study the truth in the bible and follow every command, He will help me unlock more truths to apply to my life to become closer to Him. As I give up more and more of my life for Him and allow Him into more and more of my heart, He will shine His light upon everything in my life to make sure it is straightened out to His approval. That's what I want – no compromises.

II Corinthians 6:14-18 says, "Don't become partners with those who reject God. How can you make a partnership out of right and wrong? That's not partnership; that's war. Is light best friends with dark? Does Christ go strolling with the Devil? Do trust and mistrust hold hands? Who would think of setting up pagan idols in God's holy Temple? But that is exactly what we are, each of us a temple in whom God lives. God himself put it this way: "I'll live in them, move into them; I'll be their God and they'll be my people. So leave the corruption and compromise; leave it for good," says God. "Don't link up with those who will pollute you. I want you all for myself.

I'll be a Father to you; you'll be sons and daughters to me."
The Word of the Master, God."

God gives us self-control when we walk according to His spirit; we simply need to apply it. Because of His precious Holy Spirit, we have His promise that He will dwell in us, be with us and walk among us! What more could we need? He gives us a free will to make our choices – and then blesses us with His provision, love and favor when we are obedient and choose His path. James says the prayer of a righteous man is powerful and effective. Let's keep our hearts right with Him and our prayers frequent – making sure our lives line up with His Word to bring Him glory with this one life we have, serving Him.

E. M. Bounds said (speaking of our prayer closet vs. our real life), "We must live for God out of the closet if we would meet God in the closet. It is what we are out of the closet which gives victory or brings defeat to the closet. If the spirit of the world prevails in our non-closet hours, the spirit of the world will prevail in our closet hours, and that will be a vain and idle farce."

Friends with God

"He who dwells in the shelter of the Most High will rest in the shadow of the Almighty. I will say of the LORD, "He is my refuge and my fortress, my God, in whom I trust." Surely he will save you from the fowler's snare and from the deadly pestilence." (Psalm 91:1-3)

God has been orchestrating every detail of my life since the day I was born, and even before! Last week, after several surprising conversations with friends I've known for a long time, I realized how much God has poured out His love upon me and placed me in "pleasant places" over the years (Psalm 16:5-6) "LORD, you have assigned me my portion and my cup; you have made my lot secure. The boundary lines have fallen for me in pleasant places; surely I have a delightful inheritance."

God blesses us and He is at work "behind the scenes" even when we aren't aware of it. He wants what is best for us; He never gives up on us. We may get sidetracked for a while and wallow in guilt and self-pity, but He is still there, standing by us and waiting to help us along once we realize He is our source of all things. James 1:17 says "Every good and perfect gift is from above, coming down from the Father of the heavenly lights, who does not change like shifting shadows."

We have no reason to be afraid of the future – God does not change. He said He'll never leave us nor forsake us. We need to step forward in faith, trusting Him – but first we need to sit in quietness, in His presence, waiting to hear from Him. He will guide us and direct us when we remove the distractions of this life from our surroundings and take the time to seek Him and hear His voice. We need to make Him first in our life, and that means making time for Him, with no other gods (i.e. distractions) before us. Force yourself to sit in silence and have a conversation with God – He longs for our friendship!

Friends are relationships that we give priority to and make time for. How often we make time for friends – and how often we make excuses not to sit down and really listen to God. It's easy to "talk" to Him, but real relationships require two-way communication: talking and listening. When we really focus on Him and make Him our true first priority, we find that strength and joy that we've been missing. When we are honest with God and open to hear from Him, He will share His secrets with us. Let Him bless you today – and bless Him by pressing in closer than ever before.

John 15:11-15 (MSG) - "I've told you these things for a purpose: that my joy might be your joy, and your joy wholly mature. This is my command: Love one another the way I loved you. This is the very best way to love. Put your life on the line for your friends. You are my friends when you do the things I command you. I'm no longer calling you servants because servants don't understand what their master is thinking and planning. No, I've named you friends because I've let you in on everything I've heard from the Father."

Starting Out

"So let us know, let us press on to know the Lord. His going forth is as certain as the dawn; And He will come to us like the rain, like the spring rain watering the earth." (Hosea 6:3)

When God gets our attention and we make the decision to begin to "try" a relationship with Him for the first time, we can be sure that God is pleased with that decision. He is immediately there and listening to our heart. Maybe words are difficult for us to form at first, realizing we're talking to the Creator of the entire universe. What is there that He doesn't already know? Nothing – but our relationship with Him is for our benefit, not His. We need to "relate" to Him – to talk to Him, to recognize Him, be acquainted with and understand Him – for our own good. The important thing is to be completely honest and open with Him, since He will know when we're not sincere, as He looks directly at our motives.

He is the only One who knows everything about us – He knows us better than we know ourselves – and He still loves us without condition. When we really get to know Him, we realize we can really trust Him – and His love can change everything within us! He sets everything in order – in His perfect order – in the scope of the plan He has had since the beginning of time. And the more we know Him, the more we appreciate Him, learn to hear him and immediately obey His voice and cherish Him.

Romans 10:10 says, "For with the heart a person believes (adheres to, trusts in, and relies on Christ) and so is justified (declared righteous, acceptable to God), and with the mouth he confesses (declares openly and speaks out freely his faith) and confirms [his] salvation."

We can know that God wants to spend time with us, but we need to make the decision to set aside that time to be with Him. I want to be so close to God that I am distracted from the things that I see by the things that are not seen, the things that are on God's heart. When you first fall in love with someone you can't get them off your mind – that's the kind of devotion I want to have with Jesus.

Psalm 103:1-19 says, "O my soul, bless GOD. From head to toe, I'll bless His holy name! O my soul, bless GOD, don't forget a single blessing! He forgives your sins - every one. He heals your diseases - every one. He redeems you from hell - saves your life! He crowns you with love and mercy - a paradise crown. He wraps you in goodness - beauty eternal. He renews your youth - you're always young in His presence. God makes everything come out right; He puts victims back on their feet. He showed Moses how He went about his work, opened up His plans to all Israel. God is sheer mercy and grace; not easily angered, He's rich in love. He doesn't endlessly nag and scold, nor hold grudges forever. He doesn't treat us as our sins deserve, nor pay us back in full for our wrongs. As high as heaven is over the earth, so strong is His love to those who fear Him. And as far as sunrise is from sunset,

He has separated us from our sins. As parents feel for their children, God feels for those who fear Him. He knows us inside and out, keeps in mind that we're made of mud. Men and women don't live very long; like wildflowers they spring up and blossom, But a storm snuffs them out just as quickly, leaving nothing to show they were here. God's love, though, is ever and always, eternally present to all who fear Him, Making everything right for them and their children as they follow His Covenant ways and remember to do whatever He said. God has set his throne in heaven; He rules over us all. He's the King!"

Go Higher

"Oh, that You would rend the heavens and that You would come down, that the mountains might quake and flow down at Your presence - As when fire kindles the brushwood and the fire causes the waters to boil - to make Your name known to Your adversaries, that the nations may tremble at Your presence! When You did terrible things which we did not expect, You came down; the mountains quaked at Your presence. For from of old no one has heard nor perceived by the ear, nor has the eye seen a God besides You, Who works and shows Himself active on behalf of him who [earnestly] waits for Him." (Is 64:1-4)

It is easy to live each day without really thinking about what that day represents. We fly through our activities and cross off the items on our lists. Some of us hurry through each day and others enjoy themselves at a more comfortable pace - and then we all prepare for the next day. I saw the title of a book "Why Everything You Do Today Matters Forever" and it really got my attention! We don't often live our lives accountable to anyone for our actions. We compare our lives with others so we feel good about what we've done. We bask in the accomplishments we've made, as if we ourselves have obtained this life. Some of us truly have an "abundant life" that we live. There is no personal ambition that can lay hold of the gifts God offers. We can receive them, because of what He has done, when we put God first. We know that eternity is not something we earn - it is given to us by God's great grace because of what Jesus has done for us. When we receive the truth and accept Jesus Christ as our Lord, then we receive the gift of eternal life.

Jesus said: "If you love me, you will obey what I command." (John 14:15) "Whoever has my commands and obeys them, he is the one who loves me. He who loves me will be loved by my Father, and I too will love him and show myself to him." (John 14:21) "If anyone loves me, he will obey my teaching. My Father will love him, and we will come to him and make our home with him. (John 14:23) "I no longer call you servants, because a servant does not know his master's business. Instead, I have called you friends, for everything that I learned from my Father I have made known to you." (Jn 15:15)

So often, it is apparent by our lives whether or not we really know and love our Heavenly Father. And this abundant life we find when we seriously do put God first and spend time getting to know Him will lead to eternal life. When we run after God, sincerely seeking to hear and see what's on His heart, we find that the door is already open and He stands there with His arms open wide, waiting to invite us into His presence. We were created for relationship with Him. Humbly seek Him each day and press in to know Him more - and grow up into the likeness of His son, Jesus Christ. Make every effort to see a change in your attitude as you focus on becoming more like Him. Our lives seem short and we're so easily distracted, but we have 24 hours each day to commit to the Lord and seek His wisdom and guidance for every decision we make. Let's prove that we love Him by following His commands and becoming His friend, and learn all we can about the treasures He longs to unfold before us.

D. Bonhoeffer: "Prayer does not mean simply to pour out one's heart. It means rather to find the way to God and to speak with Him, whether the heart is full or empty. No man can do that by himself. For that he needs Jesus Christ."

Moving Forward

"Then I remember something that fills me with hope. The LORD's kindness never fails! If He had not been merciful, we would have been destroyed. The LORD can always be trusted to show mercy each morning. Deep in my heart I say, "The LORD is all I need; I can depend on Him!" The LORD is kind to everyone who trusts and obeys Him. It is good to wait patiently for the LORD to save us." (Lamentations 3:21-26)

Most of the time I am quite decisive, easily making quick decisions without losing any momentum in my life; other times, however, I feel frozen or paralyzed.

Distractions constantly prevent me from focusing and way too much time passes before I force myself to make a decision. I think I am afraid to make the wrong decision, so instead I do not make any decision. I have to remind myself that even when I ask God to help me make the right decision - the one that goes along with His perfect will - I still am the one that has to make the decision and do something! An American Indian Proverb says: "Call on God, but row away from the rocks." So I have a very big part in getting things done, even after I've prayed!

Very rarely do signs drop out of the heavens directing me what to do. That's where faith comes in – and while I'm waiting for clues to the right decision, I need to hold on to hope. And at the same time, I can't wait too long, because I need to trust in love – His perfect love for me should remove any fear I might have. God wants me to do the right thing – He is not waiting to throw a lightning bolt at me when I make a wrong turn or step toward the wrong decision. And He already knows I am not perfect – who am I kidding? (Nobody.)

God is there to help us succeed because of His unfathomable love for us. When we are trying to be obedient to God, He is pleased – and when a parent is pleased with their child, they want to help the child succeed in every way possible. We just need to trust that if we start in the wrong direction, God will show us – and as we go along, take plenty of time to watch and listen for evidence of His loving hand guiding us.

We make it more difficult than it is. It takes effort, but the more you intentionally think about God throughout your day and just ask Him to help you be obedient and use you for whatever purpose He has, the easier it becomes. I love the lyrics in the song "The Motions" by Matthew West: "I don't want to go one more day without Your all-consuming passion inside of me." Let's practice that, trusting in His love and hoping for His glory while walking by faith, not sight. Let His all-consuming passion ignite inside of you... and move forward in His power.

"What folly to think that all other blessings must come from Him, but that prayer, whereon everything else depends, must be obtained by personal effort! Thank God, I begin to comprehend the Lord Jesus is himself in the inner chamber watching over me, and holding Himself responsible to teach me how to approach the Father. He only demands this – that I, with childlike confidence, wait upon Him and glorify Him." ~ A. Murray

Reflect Jesus

"And I will give you a new heart. I will give you new and right desires, and put a new Spirit within you. I will take out your stony hearts of sin and give you new hearts of love. And I will put my Spirit within you so that you will obey My laws and do whatever I command." (Ezekiel 36:26-27)

God created us with a void inside that can only be filled by Him. We tend to allow our individual tendencies to get in the way of becoming more like Him. Draw closer to God and you will become more like Him and reflect the true nature of Jesus to the world around you – that's what attracts people.

He wants to deliver us from ourselves. Do not resist, but sacrifice your natural life and become obedient to Him – He desires to lead us in the supernatural. He has higher ways for us, but He will not force Hill will upon us and change us while we resist Him. We must discipline ourselves to get rid of the old junk in our life and intentionally obey His Word. We cannot make excuses like, "Lord, You made me this way." He made us, sin transformed us into what we were, and now is the time to move on.

The gifts of the Spirit are: love, joy, peace, patience, kindness, goodness, faithfulness, gentleness and self control. Apply these to life and become a true disciple, the person God intended for you to be from the beginning.

Seek Life

"The Spirit searches all things, even the deep things of God. For who among men knows the thoughts of a man except the man's spirit within him? In the same way no one knows the thoughts of God except the Spirit of God. We have not received the spirit of the world but the Spirit who is from God, that we may understand what God has freely given us. This is what we speak, not in words taught us by human wisdom but in words taught by the Spirit, expressing spiritual truths in spiritual words. The man without the Spirit does not accept the things that come from the Spirit of God, for they are foolishness to him, and he cannot understand them, because they are spiritually discerned. The spiritual man makes judgments about all things, but he himself is not subject to any man's judgment: "For who has known the mind of the Lord that he may instruct him?" But we have the mind of Christ." (I Corinthians 2:10-16)

We have upgraded our technical navigational tools over the years – from before the time of the Titanic, from using Morse code to our current GPS units in our vehicles and on our phones. Regarding physical location, everybody wants to be heading in the right direction - and nobody enjoys being lost or wasting any time along their way. A story is told about Albert Einstein going on a train to an out-of-town engagement. Einstein frantically searched his briefcase for the ticket as the conductor waited to punch it for the ride. Finally, to avoid further frustration and delay, the conductor assured Einstein he recognized who he was, trusted he had purchased a ticket and that he could be seated. As he continued punching tickets of those in line, he glanced back to Einstein and noticed him still eagerly searching under his seat and in his pockets for the ticket. Again, he pleaded with the scientist, "I know who you are, don't worry about it." Einstein looked up and said, "I, too, know who I am. What I don't know is where I'm going."

We need to know who we are – and we need to know where we are going. The only way to go in the right direction is to talk to our Creator, to continue to develop that relationship, seeking His counsel and listening to His Spirit throughout each day. When you pray, expect an answer and take time to listen! When our thoughts are flooded with living in obedience to the plan that God had in place before our birth, we are sure to succeed! He knows your heart and has the coordinates to your perfect destination, if you will ask.

The more we think about, talk and listen to our Heavenly Father, the more our actions will follow suit and represent Him wherever we go. As we learn more of God's attributes by studying the bible we understand Him more and can follow His plan more closely. Where we spend most of our time will govern the direction we go – our thoughts become actions, which turn into habits and guide our lives. Psalms 37:4 says "Delight yourself in the Lord and He will give you the desires of your heart."

George Müller said, "The vigor of our spiritual life will be in exact proportion to the place held by the Bible in our life and thoughts."

In the Garden of Eden, the tree of life was the perfect tree. We have an obligation to seek the tree of life and lose the effects from the tree of "the knowledge of good and evil", where those who do not believe in God tend to live. Paul warns in Second Corinthians 11:3, "But I am afraid that, as the serpent deceived Eve by his craftiness, your minds will be led astray from the simplicity and purity of devotion to Christ." The tree of knowledge of good and evil is the tree of imperfection, and it led to the fall of man - the end of purity and the end of God's perfect will. The serpent that deceived Eve and convinced her to eat of the tree of knowledge of good and evil is the same "prince of the power of the air" that lives in this earth to deceive people today.

Ephesians 2:1-5 says, "It wasn't so long ago that you were mired in that old stagnant life of sin. You let the world, which doesn't know the first thing about living, tell you how to live. You filled your lungs with polluted unbelief, and then exhaled disobedience. We all did it, all of us doing what we felt like doing, when we felt like doing it, all of us in the same boat. It's a wonder God didn't lose His temper and do away with the whole lot of us. Instead, immense in mercy and with an incredible love, He embraced us. He took our sin-dead lives and made us alive in Christ." Do not allow yourself to get one degree off-course, but stay in God's will by reading the bible and enjoy His fellowship throughout each day! Revelation 2:7 says, "He who has an ear, let him hear what the Spirit says to the churches. To him who overcomes, I will give the right to eat from the tree of life, which is in the paradise of God."

Selah

"I am the vine, and you are the branches. If you stay joined to Me, and I stay joined to you, then you will produce lots of fruit. But you cannot do anything without Me." (John 15:5)

I am often reminded of the verse "apart from Me you can do nothing" (Jn 15:5) when I see people scurrying about, trying to accomplish things – and, at times, trying to escape their conscience - by being busy with "stuff" all the time. They take no time for thoughtful reflection and avoid any possibility of being alone.

Their continuous activity is similar to a hamster in its wheel – he doesn't get far, but he wears himself out with his running. People do not realize that "they're going nowhere, fast".

Throughout the Psalms, there is a word commonly placed at the end of the sentence, indicating a different lifestyle in the culture then, or at least encouraging a quieter lifestyle: "Selah" – meaning "Pause, and think about that."

Psalm 3:4 ~ To the LORD I cry aloud, and He answers me from His holy hill. Selah

Psalm 4:4 ~ In your anger do not sin; when you are on your beds, search your hearts and be silent. Selah

Psalm 24:5-6 ~ He will receive blessing from the LORD and vindication from God his Savior. Such is the generation of those who seek Him, who seek Your face, O God of Jacob. Selah

Psalm 32:5 ~ Then I acknowledged my sin to You and did not cover up my iniquity. I said, "I will confess my transgressions to the LORD" - and You forgave the guilt of my sin. Selah

Just gleaning from the verses above, let's consider how God answers you when you take the time to really cry out to Him and wait for His answer. Think about what's in your heart. Think about God and how He feels when you desire to be near Him, seeking His face; talk to God about any actions you've taken that bother you, realizing He will forgive you completely when you ask Him to – just think about that! He always follows through with the promises He has made!

It's good for us to take more time in silence and consider our daily activities – to think about any "lessons" we may derive from looking at our life, and even the lives of others. It doesn't take a rocket scientist to see the ramifications of some of the decisions that are made in the world around us today. As people make choices and the results of their decisions play out over the years, we can see a trend: God's Word (the bible) is true! The principles stand forever and the laws written within it cannot be changed by mankind.

Regardless of whether or not you agree with the Ten Commandments, the blessings and curses that follow are apparent when the choice is made to obey or not to obey. I have found life is much easier when I commit to being obedient to God's Word. It's not there to make us miserable or to add more rules to life – it is truth, and like a benefits manual, it outlines the good things that come from a life that is lived out while walking with our Creator, talking to God, spending time considering our ways and praying about what He would have us do. Just like branches are supported by the vine, we need to be dependent on Jesus, staying true to His direction, joined with Him in purpose - and watch the fruit grow!

Psalm 32:6-7 says, "For this [forgiveness] let everyone who is godly pray - pray to You in a time when You may be found; surely when the great waters [of trial] overflow, they shall not reach [the spirit in] him. You are a hiding place for me; You, Lord, preserve me from trouble, You surround me with songs and shouts of deliverance. Selah [pause, and calmly think of that]!"

Simplify

"You've always been great toward me - what love! You snatched me from the brink of disaster! ... You, O God, are both tender and kind, not easily angered, immense in love, and you never, never quit." (Ps 86:13, 15)

God has already prepared today for me! And He has prepared me for today! Not only is this a custom-made day, but God has promised never to leave me or forsake me, so He is here with me to help me face whatever comes my way!

I heard an interview on the radio recently with a musician who had just been to Kenya with Compassion International. He was talking about the culture, economy and morale in Kenya and the hopelessness he saw in the faces of people there - until he got within the walls of the "Compassion International" organization. The young people who were connected with Compassion International had an entirely different appearance: their eyes were radiant with joy, their countenance was lifted and they had hope! He was surprised that their prayers included some of the same words we pray: "Thank You, Heavenly Father, for all the blessings You give us." The difference is that when we pray those words, we're usually referring to our homes, cars, jobs, abundance, etc. They are thankful for the gift of salvation, a roof over their heads, the peace and joy they have and the love they feel - their hope is in Jesus.

So often we are distracted by the many things that we have, we take for granted the most important thing: God's gift of salvation to us through a relationship with Jesus, His love for us and His provision, the peace He offers and the joy that strengthens us when we know Him.

We have to simplify our lives and make time to commune with Jesus - He will "restore your soul". He gives us the fellowship we need, the vision to fulfill our purpose and hope as He provides us with direction. Only as we spend time with Him can He speak to our heart so we have the wisdom to go forward, in the right direction and in His strength. Let Jesus lift the confusion and chaos and lead you into the path He has planned for you - His yoke is easy, His burden is light.

A. W. Tozer once said, "We Christians must simplify our lives or lose untold treasures on earth and in eternity. Modern civilization is so complex as to make the devotional life all but impossible. The need for solitude and quietness was never greater than it is today."

In John 17:13-19, Jesus prays to His Heavenly Father, "Now I'm returning to You. I'm saying these things in the world's hearing so My people can experience My joy completed in them. I gave them Your word; the godless world hated them because of it, because they didn't join the world's ways, just as I didn't join the world's ways. I'm not asking that You take them out of the world but that You guard them from the Evil One. They are no more defined by the world than I am defined by the world.

Make them holy-consecrated-with the truth; Your word is consecrating truth. In the same way that You gave Me a mission in the world, I give them a mission in the world. I'm consecrating Myself for their sakes so they'll be truth-consecrated in their mission."

Talking to God

"Don't bargain with God. Be direct. Ask for what you need. This is not a cat-and-mouse, hide-and-seek game we're in. If your little boy asks for a serving of fish, do you scare him with a live snake on his plate? If your little girl asks for an egg, do you trick her with a spider? As bad as you are, you wouldn't think of such a thing – you're at least decent to your own children. And don't you think the Father who conceived you in love will give the Holy Spirit when you ask Him?" (Luke 11:10-13)

We, who have recognized Jesus as our Savior and asked Him to be Lord of our life, have the significant privilege of asking for His help in this life. The bible was given for our benefit today! It is not a list of rules to follow in life to make us miserable, but it is a "benefits manual" for those who love the Lord with all their heart (Deut 6:5-6) and obey Him. If you want to know how to get ahead in life, just pray for wisdom on a regular basis. The Holy Spirit is our counselor and teaches us all things – if we will ask. Study the Lord's prayer and what He teaches about prayer in Matthew 6, and see that God wants a deeper relationship with you. Continually strive to know Him more – and challenge yourself to believe He loves you more than you ever thought before – because He does! And just when you think you can grasp how great His love for you is, think again – He loves you more than you can imagine.

He gives without limit – so continue to expand your understanding of His completely unconditional love for you. We cannot fathom how much He loves us. In John 17, Jesus prays for His disciples (that's us) and gives us a great example of how a relationship with God helps us to pray for others and bless people we don't even know! John 17:20 says, "My prayer is not for them alone. I pray also for those who will believe in Me through their message, that all of them may be one, Father, just as You are in Me and I am in You. May they also be in Us so that the world may believe that You have sent Me." Pray to your Heavenly Father knowing He loves you and wants to draw closer to you and you will be amazed at how real God becomes to you, how much He loves you and how closely He will relate to you. We have no idea how much power is available when we tap into prayer, especially prayer in unity with others and with God's will.

No other relationship will replace what we are supposed to have with our Heavenly Father. There is only one God – the One who created the heavens and the earth… and each of us. And He created us for the sole purpose of having a relationship with us. I constantly try to replace that relationship with other people – finding fulfillment in a close relationship with another person. No person is able to meet all my needs – no human being is perfect enough to be the "perfect friend" – only Jesus has that ability. He knows everything about us and still loves us unconditionally. That's because He knows what sin does to people – we're all imperfect. We've all been hurt – and that hurt seeps out of us into our relationships from time to time and we unintentionally hurt those we love the most. That's why we're called to love our enemies – we're not actually fighting against other people. We all have this in common – we want to love others and we want to be loved. That desire was placed in us by our Creator, God. But only He can love us perfectly, because He has not been touched by sin. Sin was brought on by the enemy of our souls – we were created in the image of God, so our enemy wants to destroy us. He comes to kill, steal and destroy – by the power of sin in life. We all see effects of sin, because the enemy of our soul is the prince of the power of the air. We live our life quietly, in continual communion with our Heavenly Father and then live out the behavior that Jesus taught in our relationships with other human beings – but remaining focused on understanding God's presence with us.

Whatsoever ye do, do all to the glory of God. (I Corinthians 10:31)

The Priority of Prayer

"The first thing I want you to do is pray. Pray every way you know how, for everyone you know. Pray especially for rulers and their governments to rule well so we can be quietly about our business of living simply, in humble contemplation. This is the way our Savior God wants us to live. He wants not only us but everyone saved, you know, everyone to get to know the truth we've learned: that there's one God and only one, and one Priest-Mediator between God and us – Jesus, who offered Himself in exchange for everyone held captive by sin, to set them all free. Eventually the news is going to get out. This and this only has been my appointed work: getting this news to those who have never heard of God, and explaining how it works by simple faith and plain truth." (I Timothy 2:1-7)

Meet with God each morning to fill up with the knowledge of what He desires, so you can overflow to others – let your heart beat with God's heart. Seek Him each day to see where there are needs specifically designed for you to fill in the gap. Then allow the fruit of the Spirit to be manifest in your daily activities. James tell us the earnest prayer of a righteous man makes tremendous power available (James 4:16). So as you feel the Holy Spirit prompting you to pray for others, be obedient. Let the joy and love spill over into the lives of those you run into and lift up those within your sphere of influence to your

Heavenly Father. Encourage one another and challenge others to draw closer in their relationship with Jesus. You will never regret learning more about your Creator and sharing that with others – just imagine your joy when you see Him face to face knowing you were used to draw others to Him.

"As white snowflakes fall quietly and thickly on a winter day, answers to prayer will settle down upon you at every step you take, even to your dying day. The story of your life will be the story of prayer and answers to prayer." - O. Hallesby

Trusting

"How blessed the man You train, God, the woman You instruct in Your Word, providing a circle of quiet within the clamor of evil, while a jail is being built for the wicked. God will never walk away from His people, never desert His precious people. Rest assured that justice is on its way and every good heart put right." (Psalm 94:12-15)

I often find that certain times of the year lend themselves to repeatedly bringing me to a point of self-reflection. Deer hunting season is one of those times. As I sit in my tree, I tend to analyze my heart in greater depth than I normally allow time for - and I have a silent conversation with God about things that have gone neglected for too long. It seems like the longer I wait for a huge "thirty-point buck" to emerge from the woods, the more intense my reflection and the deeper my heartfelt repentance gets. Sports has the same effect on me – I (wrongly) tend to associate "victory" with being "worthy" and a "defeat" with sin somewhere in my life. In Jesus' day, the disciples responded similarly to the observations they made: "As he went along, he saw a man blind from birth. His disciples asked him, "Rabbi, who sinned, this man or his parents, that he was born blind?" (John 9:1-2)

As we look around the world today, we see plenty of "signs" that might cause us to reflect inwardly and seek forgiveness in order to turn things around toward a brighter picture around us. I think it's always a good habit to take time for reflection, but I also think there are times we need to trust that God is really with us, He will provide for us, His mercies are new every morning, He will protect us. Tumultuous times surround us in this world, but our faith causes us to look up! (Luke 21:28)

The words that we speak should be different than what others are saying – we know our God will deliver us from whatever threatens to harm us when we are right with Him! (Lamentations 3:25) "The Lord is good to those who depend on Him, to those who search for Him." We need to continually probe for greater truths from Him and listen closely to what He may speak into our hearts, to "search for Him" and to pursue Him with everything within us.

Our trust is in God, so our attitudes should reflect confidence, abundance, reaching out and ministering generously to others! We have no reason to fear because we know that God is on our side! And when we consider what Jesus went through for our benefit, we are compelled to remain steadfast. Hebrews 12:3 says, "Consider Him who endured such opposition from sinful men, so that you will not grow weary and lose heart." Jesus patiently endured questioning, ridicule, torture and death for us! God sees what is happening on the earth and His promises are still true! Enlarge your faith and may that faith be evident by the words we speak and the actions we participate in! "Then Jesus told his disciples, 'If any want to become my followers, let them deny themselves and take up their cross and follow me.'" (Matt. 16:24)

Final words (i.e. most important words)

Matthew 11:28-30, "Are you tired? Worn out? Burned out on religion? Come to Me. Get away with Me and you'll recover your life. I'll show you how to take a real rest. Walk with Me and work with Me - watch how I do it. Learn the unforced rhythms of grace. I won't lay anything heavy or ill-fitting on you. Keep company with Me and you'll learn to live freely and lightly."

As I wrap up this book, I am reminded of the quote I heard recently saying that the most important writing in a book comes last during the process of writing it. Apparently, that is true – what I want to articulate in my closing thoughts reflect my original purpose in writing this book. I'm also reminded of a conversation I had with a friend of mine shortly before he passed away. He shared his appreciation for my friendship, and since it sounded like a farewell, I didn't want to hear it at the time – but now that he's no longer here on earth, I cherish the words he shared with me that day. So often, the parting words of friends and family become the most important and comforting words we remember. So before I bring this book to a close, allow me to share some parting words.

The articles in this book started out as journal entries – little lessons I'd think of while driving down the road or thoughts throughout the day. Often I'd hear of someone struggling with a situation and think of a similar

Karmen Asch

experience, sometimes one I had already written about. I began to consider the value of sharing my thoughts and perspective to others - revealing another view of a tough situation or perhaps a more optimistic way of looking at things. Seeing a problem or solution from different angles helps us figure out the best way to handle things in life. I especially like seeing life on earth from a higher standpoint – from an unchanging Advisor. I think prayer gave me that "leverage" early on in life and I want others to benefit from that tool to make life easier along this journey.

Two things I've learned are true – but seemingly contradict one another in this life. Number one: we were created for relationships – we crave friendship with others, as hard as relationships prove to be over time. Number two: people will always disappoint us – the longer we know someone, the more likely it becomes that they will offend us with something they say or do. And yet, we continue to build relationships throughout our lives.

But I'll share a third truth I've learned: my Heavenly Father never disappoints – the relationship grows more and more fulfilling and yet remains an endless pursuit of wanting more of Him, more of the truth. It leads to more joy and peace, a greater ability to love others over time and also yields greater understanding and wisdom along the way.

Sometimes as we get older, it's easy to become discouraged more often. Like Damian Hirst, we think: "Why do I feel so important when I'm not? Nothing is important and everything is important. I do not know why I am here but I am glad that I am. I'd rather be here than not. I am going to die and I want to live forever, I can't escape that fact, and I can't let go of that desire."

With the loss of loved ones and exposure to all the hurt and pain in this world, we can begin to feel empty inside – to wonder, "Have I been dealt a bad hand? Is some distant deity playing games with my life? Does it really matter what I do – will my actions truly determine how my life ends? Is this really just a 'chasing after the wind'?"

Most of the time when I'm discouraged, I realize it's because I get too busy with "life", the cares of this world, and neglect that relationship with my Heavenly Father – and it ultimately leads to me feeling frustrated about everything and desperately crying out to Him to "fix" all the situations falling apart around me. And He is always right there – spot on – with just the right words (not audibly, but mysteriously - organizing my thoughts, speaking to my heart with truths, mostly simple things that are profound in their timeliness) to bring that peace of mind I need once more. Many times, I end up laughing at myself for getting frustrated in the first place as I see how simple it is to just throw everything at His feet and quit trying to control things myself. He is so much better at it! I love these verses from King Solomon, the wisest man to ever live: (Ecclesiastes, MSG)

7:14 – "On a good day, enjoy yourself; On a bad day,

examine your conscience. God arranges for both kinds of days so that we won't take anything for granted."

7:29 – "One discovery...I didn't find one man or woman in a thousand worth my while. Yet I did spot one ray of light in this murk: God made men and women true and upright; we're the ones who've made a mess of things."

8:12-13 – "Even though a person sins and gets by with it hundreds of times throughout a long life, I'm still convinced that the good life is reserved for the person who fears God, who lives reverently in His presence, and that the evil person will not experience a "good" life. No matter how many days he lives, they'll all be as flat and colorless as a shadow - because he doesn't fear God."

9:7-10 ~ "Seize life! Eat bread with gusto, drink wine with a robust heart. Oh yes - God takes pleasure in your pleasure! Dress festively every morning. Don't skimp on colors and scarves. Relish life with the spouse you love each and every day of your precarious life. Each day is God's gift. It's all you get in exchange for the hard work of staying alive. Make the most of each one! Whatever turns up, grab it and do it - and heartily! This is your last and only chance at it, for there's neither work to do nor thoughts to think in the company of the dead, where you're most certainly headed."

(11:1-10) "Be generous: Invest in acts of charity. Charity yields high returns. Don't hoard your goods; spread them around. Be a blessing to others. This could be your last night. When the clouds are full of water, it rains. When the wind blows down a tree, it lies where it falls. Don't sit there watching the wind. Do your own work. Don't stare at the clouds. Get on with your life. Just as you'll never understand the mystery of life forming in a pregnant woman, so you'll never understand the mystery at work in all that God does. Go to work in the morning and stick to it until evening without watching the clock. You never know from moment to moment how your work will turn out in the end. Oh, how sweet the light of day, and how wonderful to live in the sunshine! Even if you live a long time, don't take a single day for granted. Take delight in each light-filled hour, remembering that there will also be many dark days and that most of what comes your way is smoke. You who are young, make the most of your youth. Relish your youthful vigor. Follow the impulses of your heart. If something looks good to you, pursue it. But know also that not just anything goes; you have to answer to God for every last bit of it. Live footloose and fancy-free - you won't be young forever. Youth lasts about as long as smoke."

When the monotony of everyday life begins to pry at your heart and your imagination begins to question the purpose of it all, look up! Cry out – and know that God is very near! There is one Who created all of this for a purpose – and for a good purpose! We can't see the big picture yet, so we need to lean on faith, trusting Him. Nietzsche once said: "He who has a 'why' to live for can bear almost any 'how'." Trust God to give you the "why". He will give you a life of abundance as you begin to put your trust in Him - as you begin a relationship with Him. It's as simple as saying a few sincere words to the One who created you with more love than you could ever imagine:

"Heavenly Father, I'm not sure about this – but I want to be sure. I want to believe that there is more to life than meets the eye. Show me Your hand of love at work in my life. Help me to understand Your plan for my life and see it unfolding throughout life's circumstances so I know You are real. I want to know and feel Your unconditional love for me. I'm sorry that I haven't trusted in You before now, but I'm asking for Your grace and mercy to wash over me and give me a new start in life – forgive me. Open my eyes and let me see things differently. You know everything about me – I'm asking You to help me hear You as You speak to my heart about personal decisions I need to make. I receive Your invitation to follow You. I will obey You as You provide clear direction for me. Thank You for Your love for me, for Your willingness to forgive everything I've done and for Your clear direction as I step forward by faith."

Romans 10:4-10 says, "The earlier revelation was intended simply to get us ready for the Messiah, who then puts everything right for those who trust Him to do it. Moses wrote that anyone who insists on using the law code to live right before God soon discovers it's not so easy - every detail of life regulated by fine print! But trusting God to shape the right living in us is a different story - no precarious climb up to heaven to recruit the Messiah, no dangerous descent into hell to rescue the Messiah. So what exactly was Moses saying? 'The word that saves is right here, as near as the tongue in your mouth, as close as the heart in your chest.' It's the word of faith that welcomes God to go to work and set things right for us. This is the core of our preaching. Say the welcoming word to God – 'Jesus is my Master' - embracing, body and soul, God's work of doing in us what He did in raising Jesus from the dead. That's it. You're not "doing" anything; you're simply calling out to God, trusting Him to do it for you. That's salvation. With your whole being you embrace God setting things right, and then you say it, right out loud: **'God has set everything right between Him and me!'"**

About the Author

Karmen's years of growing up on a small farm in Edenville, MI, gave her an endless cache of hands-on experience with small farm animals, birds, insects, amphibians and reptiles that she loved during her childhood - and many frogs and snakes were collected temporarily as pets, to her brother's dismay. By tapping into the wonders of nature, Karmen weaves them into articles containing lessons for living life well.

The creation of nature's intricate beauty reflects the Father's heart. Karmen's immense appreciation of all that God's heart created is reflected through her articles. Integrating her unique analogies with her photography, she has designed an amazing book with built-in wisdom for an enjoyable reading experience, as well as unique perspectives we can learn from.

Karmen works at Dow Corning Corporation in Midland, Michigan. She began in 1989 as a co-op her senior year at Meridian High School and continued her education at Central Michigan University, Saginaw Valley and Delta. Karmen lives in Gladwin County with her husband, Steve, on a small farm originally belonging to Steve's Grandpa Lee. They have horses and enjoy gardening. They also like riding their Harleys, going fishing and camping up north, and enjoy time spent with their granddaughters, Katy and Abby. Karmen enjoys playing pool; she also loves music, birds, cross-country skiing, photography, bonfires and hikes through the woods.

LaVergne, TN USA
21 September 2010
197754LV00001B/1/P

9 781449 011246